# Treating Sexually Abused Children
## and
## their Families

# Treating Sexually Abused Children
## and
## their Families

*Beverly James, L.C.S.W.,*
*and*
*Maria Nasjleti, L.C.S.W.*

CONSULTING PSYCHOLOGISTS PRESS, INC.
577 College Ave., Palo Alto, CA 94306

Editor:    Ann Margulies
Production Coordinator:    Ann Wood
Copy Editor:    Amy Klatzkin
Text Designer:    Judy Olson
Cover Designer:    Spectra Media
Composition:    Dharma Press

**Library of Congress Cataloging in Publication Data**

James, Beverly, 1939–
    Treating sexually abused children and their families.

    Bibliography: p.
    1. Sexually abused children.    2. Family psychotherapy.
I. Nasjleti, Maria, 1948–    .    II. Title.
HQ71.J34    1983    362.7′044    83-15433
ISBN 0-89106-023-5

Printed in the United States of America

ISBN 0-89106-023-5

The profile of male incest victims includes information adapted from Maria Nasjleti, "Suffering in Silence: The Male Incest Victim," *Child Welfare* 59, no. 5 (May 1980): pp. 267–75; adapted by special permission of the Child Welfare League of America.

# Table of Contents

Describes sexually abused children, indicators of sexual abuse, profiles of male and female victims.

Presents profiles of sexual abusers of children: male in parent role, "friendly neighborhood molester," the boy next door, women as molesters.

Presents profiles of mothers of incest victims: the passive child-woman mother; the intelligent, competent, distant mother; the rejecting, vindictive mother; the psychotic or severely retarded mother.

Presents sexual abuse of children as a generational phenomenon; describes family constellation, family members' parts in abusive system, family reaction.

# *Preface*

Despite the increasing awareness of the destructive effects of sexual abuse of children, there have been few definitive, clear models that professionals can use to order the work that needs to be done. In *Treating Sexually Abused Children and their Families,* Beverly James and Maria Nasjleti provide a carefully designed and effective intervention system that can help professionals in many fields to work with both the victim of sexual abuse and the victimizer.

The clarity of the book allows us all—professionals in the fields of child education, psychology, social work, juvenile justice, and parent education—to understand clearly the task before us. Objective criteria for assessing the results of our work are succinctly and carefully outlined. A sequence of therapeutic interventions, valuable notes on the techniques and skills needed, and an encyclopedia of eclectic approaches to difficult issues combine to make this small book very large and significant in scope, depth, and value.

The presence of a coherent treatment plan for families engaged in sexual abuse allows those responsible for making legal decisions to be aware that a feasible plan of action exists: that rehabilitation may be as viable a choice as the long-term removal of the child or the abuser from the family or the incarceration of the abuser.

This book arises from the experiences of two therapists who have demonstrated effectiveness in their work and who now offer it as a guide to others. We believe it can and should be a positive force in helping to reduce the destructive effects of sexual abuse. We are thankful to both Beverly and Maria for sharing their sensitivity and their concern for our children.

Jacqueline Kelley-Kinnie, M.A., M.S.      Ernest J. Kinnie, Ph.D.
Educational Psychologist      Clinical Psychologist

# About the Authors

BEVERLY JAMES, state of California licensed Social Worker, received her Masters Degree of Social Work at the University of Hawaii and her Certificate of Advanced Study in International Social Work from the East-West Center. After serving as a United Nations Intern in Bangkok, she did two years' postmasters study at the California Graduate School of Marital and Family Therapy. The author of a number of publications, Ms. James has also taught in Micronesia, worked as a family therapist for Child Welfare Services, and was coordinator of an evaluation program for emotionally disturbed children at Children's Gardens in Marin County. She currently conducts workshops and seminars dealing with sexually abused children throughout the state of California and is a member of the National Speakers Association. She has a private family therapy practice in Point Richmond, California.

MARIA NASJLETI did her undergraduate work at the University of Michigan. She moved to California in 1971 and completed her Masters in Social Work at California State University, Sacramento, in 1974. She worked for five years in Child Welfare Services in Sacramento, California, where she became interested in developing a comprehensive treatment program for sexually abusive families. In 1978, she was one of the founding members of the Sacramento Child Sexual Abuse Treatment Program, where she was Clinical Program Coordinator until 1981. In 1979, she became a faculty member in the California State University, Sacramento, School of Social Work. She has continued her clinical training at the California Graduate School of Marital and Family Therapy. Since 1980, Ms. Nasjleti has been a clinical social worker for the Pediatrics Ward at Stanford University Hospital, where she works with critically and chronically ill children and their families. She continues to be a consultant in child sexual abuse and speaks regularly at conferences and seminars on child abuse. Her current teaching, research, and clinical work focuses on the support of parents and chronically ill children.

# Acknowledgments

We wish to acknowledge the professional editorial skills of Janna Patee, who took on the formidable task of blending our two writing styles.

Numerous friends, colleagues, and adversaries have assisted in our clinical growth. We thank them sincerely and particularly appreciate the contributions of:

Sandra Baker, L.C.S.W.
Candace Diamond, M.A.
Patricia Dixon, M.D.
William Hunt, L.C.S.W.
Martin Kirschenbaum, Ph.D.
Kenneth Peterson, Esq.
Gladys Rosenblum, M.S.W.
Morgan Smith, M.F.C.C.
Hon. Sandra Smith
Sue Tuana, L.C.S.W.
Sandra Wilhoit, M.S.W.
Marie Witt, Ph.D.
Norman Main, Esq.
Sacramento County Juvenile Probation Department

A special thank-you to Consulting Psychologists Press and our skilled and enthusiastic editor, Ann Margulies, who helped to make a dream a reality.

# Introduction

The sexual abuse of children came to be recognized as a significant form of child maltreatment during the 1970s in this country. Earlier, Kinsey and his colleagues (1948, 1953) found that 25 percent of American women and 10 percent of American men had been sexually assaulted before age eighteen. Studies based on reported cases underestimate the frequency of occurrence, but they do show an increasing frequency. A study published in 1955 estimated the rate of abuse at 1.9 per million people per year (Weinberg 1955), but more recent research has reported much higher rates: In 1968, the American Humane Association estimated the rate at 40 per million per year (DeFrancis 1968a), and in 1983 that organization reported the 1980 figures as 53 *reported* cases per million children under eighteen (American Humane Association 1983).

The recognition of the fact that great numbers of people are involved in this deviant behavior has helped to bring the problem to the attention of public educators. Passage of the Federal Child Abuse Prevention and Treatment Act of 1974 gave national legal attention to the phenomenon. Associations of mental health professionals, law enforcement officials, and juvenile court authorities have embraced the subject as an important topic for study and discussion. The consciousness of the average person has been raised with respect to sexual abuse of children by television and other media reports ranging from Phil Donahue's interviews with an abuse victim and her parents to documentaries about child prostitution in New York City to Congressional hearings on child pornography. Although incest and sexual abuse remain strict taboos, discussion of the problem no longer is.

The operational definition of what constitutes sexual abuse of children is largely a matter of jurisdictional and individual interpretation by the several states and their subdivisions. Legal definitions make distinctions based on a victim's age, the relationship of the abuser, and the getting of financial profit from an indirect participation in such abuse, as well as what has actually been done to a child. The definition of sexual abuse that we consider the broadest and most accurate is that adopted by the National Center on Child Abuse and Neglect:

> Contacts or interactions between a child and an adult when the child is being used for the sexual stimulation of the perpetrator or another person. Sexual abuse may also be committed by a person under the age of 18 when that person is either significantly older than the victim or when the perpetrator is in a position of power or control over another child.*

Since the acceptance of sexual abuse of children as a problem of sufficient magnitude to demand governmental concern and treatment programs in human service programs, a number of papers, monographs, and books have appeared to document the prevalence of sexual abuse. However, few textbooks outline characteristics that are peculiar in the development of the problem or describe the treatment phases that are in some significant ways different from those associated with other problems of social and mental health. And although therapists and workshop participants frequently pursue educators and writers with requests for "recipes" for helping victims and perpetrators of sexual abuse, specific interventions are rarely prescribed.

Butler (1978) and Sgroi (1982) view the power and authority of the male offender as the crucial components in sexual abuse of children within the family unit. We agree that power and authority play significant roles in intrafamilial abuse. However, we view these elements as only some of a number of necessary individual and familial dynamics that permit child sexual abuse to continue over a period of time. In short, we view intrafamilial child sexual

---

*Child Sexual Abuse: Incest, Assault, and Sexual Exploitation. A special report from the National Center on Child Abuse and Neglect, U.S. Department of Health, Education and Welfare, Washington, D.C., 1978, p. 2.

abuse as a symptom of family dysfunction and not solely as a misuse of authority and power.

It is our belief that the people involved in sexual abuse situations are the products of systems that can be defined and described in ways that are distinguishable from other patterns of social deviance. Consequently, we are also convinced that the treatment phases should differ from those used to structure other situations. Because of these beliefs, we offer specific, clinically validated intervention techniques that have helped both abusers and abused. We also point out the professional and personal skills and qualities that the therapist needs in order to work effectively with problems of sexual abuse.

# Part One

## Family Dynamics

The availability of more articles in the professional literature, increased clinical research, and more documented case examples dealing with the myriad problems of child sexual abuse have positively affected the work of clinicians. In spite of this, misconceptions continue to exist in the professional community, such as:

- Sexual abuse victims have premorbid personalities.
- Boys are not often victims.
- Infants and toddlers are not victims.
- Women are not victimizers.
- There is no potential for change in a sexually abusive family.
- Short-term therapy for intrafamilial sexual abuse is effective.
- Girls make up stories and fantasize about having sex with adults.
- Mothers who are not aware of the child sexual abuse in the family have no responsibility for it.
- Usually only one child in the family is sexually abused.
- Sexual molestation of a child by an adult is not necessarily harmful.

Our clinical experience, based on seven years of therapeutic work with sexually abusive families, dispells these misconceptions.

Part 1 of this book describes the characteristics of boys and girls who are victims, the indicators of sexual abuse, profiles of men and women who victimize or who are passive participants, and the generational cycle of sexual abuse. It also describes in detail the dynamics of male incest victims as originally reported in 1980 by Nasjleti. This report continues to provide professionals with insight into the unique dynamics of male incest victims.

Mothers of incest victims have not been described in the professional literature with regard to their individual differences. Our clinical experience has enabled us to delineate four distinct behavior patterns in women within sexually abusive families. These are outlined and discussed in Chapter 3.

The professional literature describes the generational cycle for other forms of child abuse—emotional, physical, and psychological. Yet nowhere could we find a discussion of how it comes into existence within sexually abusive families or how it is perpetuated. In our training of other professionals, we found that for them to establish a theoretical base, it was crucial that they understand the unique aspects of the generational cycle of sexual abuse. The cycle of child sexual abuse is described in terms of the parents' vulnerability to participate in this type of behavior as a function of the dynamics of their family of origin. Our clinical findings validate the family systems theory found in the writings of Satir, Haley, Jackson, Bowen, and others.

We are hopeful that the reader will obtain a broader view and gain a deeper understanding of both the individual and family dynamics involved in child molestation. For therapists who have dealt with child sexual abuse, this part of the book provides a review and validates their own experiences.

*Chapter One*

# The Molested Child

The victims of child sexual abuse are infants, toddlers, children, and teenagers. They are male, and they are female. They are victims because they are helpless—easily exploited, bribed, and coerced. They do not tell because of their shame and a sense of loyalty to their parents.

The effects of the sexual abuse of children range from nightmares to suicide. The degree of harm depends on the frequency, duration, intensity, and nature of the acts; the child's developmental stage of growth; the child's relationship to the victimizer; and the family and community's support of the child when the sexual abuse is reported.

A number of writers endorse the notion that sexual acts between adults and children are not necessarily harmful. It has been our experience that these acts are not engaged in for the benefit of the child but rather for adult sexual gratification. Any act that would contribute to or cause the following is, we believe, harmful to the child's development:

- Loss of childhood innocence
- Alienation from peers
- Inability to cope with the power of an adult in a lover role
- Pressure on the child for being singled out from siblings and peers as special
- The burden of keeping a relationship secret from others
- The experience of emotions too powerful to be worked through with a child's mental mechanisms
- Overloading stimulation and insufficient tension relief
- Forming an alliance with one parent against another

Whether a child masters an early experience or is made more vulnerable because of that experience is not obvious until later. Long-term effects of experiences are known only in retrospect. There is no evidence that sexual relationships between an adult and a child contribute to the well-being of the child or family. We believe, therefore, that it is in the best interests of the child to assume that such experiences are damaging.

## INDICATORS OF CHILD SEXUAL ABUSE

None of the following behaviors in and of themselves indicates that a child is an incest victim, but two or more indicators should alert the professional to this possibility and the need to explore the situation with the child.

1. **Excessive masturbation.** Excessive masturbation is not only symptomatic of an extraordinary interest in the child's own sexuality but may also be a subconsciously motivated practice aimed at calling others' attention to the abusive situation. It is clearly a symbolic signal that there is something inappropriate in the child's psychosexual development. Additionally, a child may masturbate constantly to relieve the itch and discomfort of a venereal disease.
2. **Overt sexual acting-out toward adults.** Adults who molest children often tell them that sex between adults and children is a permissible and accepted way of showing love. Incest victims therefore often make sexual advances toward adults they like because they have been taught that it is appropriate and because they have come to associate nurturance with sexuality through their molestation experiences. They believe that they must provide sexual gratification to adults in order to receive love.
3. **Simulation of sophisticated sexual activity with younger children.** Although boys and girls may not acknowledge that their molestation of younger children is done in an effort to communicate their own victimization to persons outside their family, it is our contention that their behavior is subconsciously motivated toward this end.

4. **Fear of being alone with an adult, either male or female.** Children who have been molested have often been told by the molester that they are irresistible, and they come to believe that all adults will be unable to control the impulse to molest them.

5. **Violence against younger children.** Incest victims cannot safely express the anger and frustration they feel toward the molesting adult and will displace these feelings onto safer objects, such as younger children. They may also displace anger onto "safe" adults, such as teachers.

6. **Self-mutilation.** Child victims often develop feelings of self-hatred related to their powerlessness to defend themselves from incestuous assaults. This loss of self-respect may be expressed in self-abusive behaviors such as tattooing or putting cigarette burns on their arms.

7. **Bruises and hickeys or both in the face or neck area or around the groin, buttocks, and inner thighs.** It is not unusual for incest victims to have numerous bruises or hickeys on their bodies, administered during molestation incidents. Often the bruises are a result of violence in response to the child's resisting the assault, and the hickeys may demonstrate varying degrees of redness, indicating that they were not all administered at the same time.

8. **Fear of bathrooms and showers.** Incest victims are frightened of bathrooms and showers because these are the places where they are most often molested. Under the pretense of helping the child with his or her bath, parents and relatives often use such opportunities to molest the child.

9. **Knowledge of sexual matters and details of adult sexual activity inappropriate to age or developmental level.** Children who are being molested are not aware of the uniqueness of their experience, often because the molesters tell them incest occurs in all families. There is only one way children learn the details of sophisticated adult sexual activity, and that is by having experienced it.

10. **Combination of violence and sexuality in artwork, written schoolwork, language, and play.** Children experience being molested as violence even when they are not physically injured. They therefore express a great deal of anger and pain in describing it, whether in words, art, or play. Molested children report having communicated their incest problem to teachers

and others in their schoolwork, honestly expecting that adult professionals would interpret their messages requesting help.

11. **Extreme fear or repulsion when touched by an adult of either sex.** Incest victims do not associate a nurturing touch with pleasure or safety. Such touching has been foreplay for them, or what has led up to molestation situations. Being touched affectionately by an adult is therefore unlikely to be pleasurable; rather, it is threatening and terrifying.

12. **Refusal to undress for physical education class at school.** Incest victims believe people can tell just by looking at their bodies that they have been molested, so they are unwilling to be seen naked by others. Also, they have often been told by the molester that their bodies are irresistible and that the molester cannot keep from molesting them. The children therefore fear that if they are seen nude, other people may lose control and molest them.

## FEMALE VICTIMS

The most significant characteristic we have noted among female victims is their role in the family. They are the dominant females. They are the ones who meet the emotional needs of adults, the ones who care for the children, and often the ones who are consulted in making decisions. This role reversal and the option of telling the family secret may lead one to assume that the child has power within the family system, but this is not the case. These girls usually have many responsibilities but little power, and they are generally passive. They believe that their survival rests on their willingness and ability to parent their parents. They see themselves as self-sacrificing and useful to others; the family's problems are their responsibility.

The girls' neediness and the reinforcement of their self-sacrificing behavior keeps them in victim roles. Their pseudomaturity and their need to protect the family from pain and disruption are two of the reasons sexually assaultive behavior is not reported or the reports are greatly minimized. In police stations, hospitals, and courtrooms, girls as young as five years old will dry their mothers' tears, pat their backs, and assure them that everything will be all right. The tragedy is that the girls' needs for affection, protection, and security are neglected as they nurture their parents. Fooled by the underreporting of assaults and the victims' appearance of maturity, helping professionals often mistakenly conclude that the victims do not need therapy.

The guilt and shame that female victims experience is compounded by the occasional sexual pleasure they feel during incidents of sexual abuse. They do not understand that the sexual pleasure is an involuntary physiological response to sexual stimuli. Instead they believe that if they got pleasure they must have wanted it to happen. Their ambivalence and confusion about these incidents is therefore understandable.

In terms of appearance, sexual development, and behavior, there is little to indicate sexual-abuse victims. They are generally average girls, although there are exceptions. Some examples follow.

## Appearance

Occasionally we find a little girl dressed like Alice in Wonderland while all her peers are in jeans. Her mother looks much older than her years and is noticeably unkempt. Teenagers will sometimes show signs of gross neglect, such as rotten teeth, unwashed body and hair, and obesity. This is an attempt to ward off male attention as well as a sign of depression. Other girls seem obsessed with always being well groomed because they fear that others can tell that they are molestation victims. They believe that their bodies are smelly and rotten inside; if they keep very clean they will be able to keep this hidden.

## Sexual Development

Most girls fall within the normal range of development of secondary sex characteristics. However, we have had girls as young as ten years old who were pregnant as a result of sexual molestation; we have also worked with sixteen-year-olds in whom menarche had not occurred. What is notable about these girls sexually is their low self-image and their ignorance. At some point, they sense that what has happened to them is abhorrent to others. They are afraid to speak of sexual issues and generally do not have peer contact to check out information.

Behavior

Intellectually, most girls are within the normal range. Generally, they do not do well scholastically because they have difficulty concentrating, in addition to the other problems already mentioned. Some girls will fail in school as a cry for help to teachers and counselors. Some girls just give up. However, a small number of girls are high achievers. They compulsively work to get the highest grades and the teacher's approval. They believe that they need to compensate for their "defect."

Acting-out behavior is sometimes observed among female sexual-abuse victims. They will try to escape a sexually abusive situation by using drugs or running away. When this happens, engaging in prostitution becomes a survival mechanism. Indiscriminate sexual behavior and locker-room talk are most often counterphobic reactions. These girls push themselves into the places they most fear.

Withdrawn, placating behavior is also observed among female victims. This group will often continue to comply with the victimizer because they believe that they are protecting other children from him. And besides, they feel they "don't matter anyway."

## MALE INCEST VICTIMS*

Statistics indicate that the ratio of female incest victims to male is ten to one. Our experience is that the ratio is more like six to four. It is our belief, supported by our clinical findings, that boys do not report being sexually victimized as readily because they equate victimization with the loss or absence of masculinity.

American males are socialized to be physically aggressive, self-reliant, independent, and emotionally self-sufficient. They are not commonly given permission to express feelings of vulnerability, helplessness, fear, or pain. Males come to equate such feelings with a lack of masculinity. Understandably, they find it difficult to express fear or pain, to acknowledge vulnerability, and to ask for help. To males, being a victim means not being a "real man."

---

*The following description of the male incest victim is adapted from Maria Nasjleti's "Suffering in Silence: The Male Incest Victim," *Child Welfare* 59, no. 5 (May 1980); adapted by special permission of the Child Welfare League of America.

It is not surprising to discover that male incest victims have these feelings about reporting their own abuse. They report feeling at least ambivalence and at worst dread about identifying themselves as victims. Reporting his own sexual victimization may activate in a boy one or more of the following fears:

1. Since he was unable to protect himself, he fears being considered a sissy or unmanly. Fearing that he may be ridiculed and rejected if he identifies himself as a victim, he may choose not to risk it.
2. If he has been molested by a male, he may fear that people will think he is homosexual, since he is likely to fear becoming homosexual. Such fears arise out of boys' belief that homosexual molestation can cause homosexuality.
3. If he has been sexually abused by a woman, he may hesitate to report it if he thinks his complaint will bring his masculinity into question. Boys often assume such a complaint will be interpreted as evidence of their sexual abnormality.
4. Boys often fear that having sex with their mother is indicative of their own mental illness. Since mothers are viewed as nonsexual beings in our culture, incapable of abusing their children, boys who are molested by their mothers often assume responsibility for their own molestation.
5. Boys fear that no one will believe their report of sexual abuse; they think boy molestation is too uncommon to be believable. This fear is explained by the lack of coverage of the topic in the news media, except in the most sensational cases.
6. Boys fear reporting their own sexual abuse because asking for help makes them feel ashamed that they were unable to protect themselves.
7. Boys fear that nothing will be done to stop their sexual abuse by a woman, because they believe that most people think such sexual activity is not harmful to the boy. Television and movies, for example, often depict the sexual exploitation of boys by women as a positive, romantic experience.
8. Boys fear reporting their own sexual victimization when reporting it may mean risking their safety and well-being. This fear is based in reality, since many times relatives threaten the boys they are molesting with physical harm if the abuse is reported. Fear of injury is one of the major reasons boys wait

until they are in adolescence to report their own sexual abuse, when their size and weight allows them to feel less physically vulnerable.

Most male incest victims are molested by male relatives. However, it is our belief that mother-son or woman-boy molestation is under-reported. Our experience has been that boys do not report such molestation until after they enter treatment. One of our cultural myths is that the seduction of a male child by a female is a positive sexual experience for the boy. This is one of the reasons boys do not report such molestation.

The facts surrounding the effects of the seduction of a male child by his mother, mother surrogate, or other significant female are these:

1. Rapists are often found to have had sexual or sexualized relationships with their mothers.
2. Among boys who have sexual relationships with their mothers, those who develop mental disorders often develop schizophrenia.
3. Incestuous fathers are often found to have had sexually stimulating relationships with their mothers.
4. Some homosexuals are said to have chosen homosexuality as a defense against their sexual feelings for a seductive mother.
5. Clinical work with child molesters indicates that sexuality is not usually the primary issue involved in their molesting behavior. Sexuality is instead the arena in which psychosocial issues such as their own childhood seduction are played out.

Although boys do not commonly report incestuous assault until late puberty or early adolescence, they share some characteristics that allow us to identify them with a fair degree of accuracy. Boys are molested in the same ways as girls. They have experienced fondling, masturbation, oral copulation, and anal penetration. Often they have been forced to be the fondler, the masturbator, and the penetrator. Much of the guilt male victims experience is related to having at times responded sexually to the sexual stimulation of molestation. The fact that the human body produces sexual excitement when sexually stimulated, regardless of the stimulator's relationship, is something victims are not aware of and need to be informed of when entering treatment. Victims state that their reluctance to report the incest came partially from feeling ashamed of having at times felt aroused. The sexual arousal leads to sexual activity with peers, which, when found to be more emotionally comfortable than incest, leads to active efforts to stop the incest. Resistance to continuing the incest often leads the parent to use violence to coerce the boy into compliance. This in turn often results in injury to the boy and the eventual involvement of Children's Protective Services or other legal authorities.

Male incest victims often enter the system identified as something other than incest victims—as victims of physical abuse, as runaways, as truants, as incorrigibles, or as violent delinquents. Of all acting-out behaviors that bring a boy to the attention of juvenile authorities, the molestation of younger children has been found to be the most consistent indicator of a boy's own sexual victimization. The possibility of incestuous sexual abuse should be explored with *all* boys who have molested younger children.

## Chapter Two

# *The Victimizers*

Who are the victimizers? The victimizers we know something about are those who are caught, for the problem of child abuse is a crime and a taboo in our society. It has been our experience that the majority of people who sexually victimize children do not voluntarily come forward to ask for help in changing their behavior. As diversion treatment programs develop across the country, there have been increases in self-referrals; however, on close examination we find that even in such cases the victimizer is coerced into treatment because the victim or another person has threatened to report the abuse.

The diversion program we are most familiar with is in Sacramento County, California. Independent agencies—the District Attorney's office, which makes the initial referral; Child Protective Services or the juvenile court; and the Sacramento Child Sexual Abuse Treatment Program, directed by Sandra Baker, L.C.S.W.— work in cooperation. The program began as a federally funded project but quickly became the model for similar programs in other counties in California and now in numerous other states.

The clinical component of the Sacramento Child Sexual Abuse Treatment Program is based on the premise that there is the potential for change only in the victimizer who openly acknowledges responsibility for the sexual abuse of a child he or she is parenting. Only about one in ten reported cases of child sexual abuse are deemed appropriate for diversion into treatment. The victimizer and the spouse sign a legally binding contract written by the District Attorney that:

1. Identifies in specific terms the sexual abuses committed by the victimizer, including dates and penal-code sections violated.
2. States clearly a commitment for every family member to participate in treatment—individual, couple, group, and conjoint family therapy—for a period of two to three years, depending on the duration and severity of the sexual abuse.
3. Acknowledges that any new offenses will result in immediate prosecution of both the new offenses and all past offenses.

The contract boxes the victimizer in by not allowing any legal loopholes. This constraint is based on the belief that when given the choice between something difficult and something easy, people will generally choose the easy way out. The program therefore gives the victimizer the choice between two difficult things: going to therapy or going to jail.

Victimizers often view the legal contract as a life-saver at the time of the signing, since it enables them to escape prosecution, prevents destruction of the family, and salvages their careers. But when the crisis is over, victimizers' anger at being boxed in by the contract emerges. Their impulse is to flee treatment, but of course they cannot. Diversion treatment programs do not work without such legally binding contracts. With the use of the legal "big stick," the Sacramento program has been successful and estimates a low recidivism rate (known recurrence while in treatment) of 1 to 5 percent for the 150 families treated in four years.

Studies describing victimizers, then, are studies of those who have been caught. The studies report what is observed in the victimizers' behavior and what the victimizers say about themselves. Research in this area is certainly influenced by the settings available to the researcher. For example, studies done in prisons show more antisocial behavior; studies in residential mental-health programs show more severe ego disorientation; studies in alcohol rehabilitation programs show more substance abuse; studies in urban areas show fewer instances of abuse than do studies from rural, isolated subcultures where there may be some measure of social acceptance. Finally, new programs available to assist families tend to show the victimizer as a fairly well-functioning family man who has a problem with impulse control in this one area of sexuality. Most reported victimizers are adult males. As professionals have become aware of the seriousness of the problem of sexual abuse and of the laws requiring reporting, the reported number of female victimizers and adolescent male victimizers has increased.

Keeping in mind that each victimizer we have worked with in clinical practice is a complex individual with unique experiences, background, attitudes, values, and involvement in a family system and a social milieu, we roughly categorize the victimizers, profiling some similarities we have observed. The groups we will describe, from most often to least often reported, are sibling incest victimizers, men in a parental role, the friendly neighborhood molester, the boy next door, and women in a parental role.

## SIBLING INCEST VICTIMIZERS

Sibling incest is reported in the literature as the most common form of incest and supposedly the least emotionally and psychologically damaging or traumatic (Arndt and Ladd, 1976; Weeks, 1976; Lukianowicz, 1972). Some researchers have asserted that sibling incest is not truly harmful because it occurs between persons of about the same age and emotional development. It has been our experience that sibling incest most often occurs in families where an adult is sexually abusive. We have seen it in families where the role boundaries are confused or nonexistent. Children who become sexually active with siblings may be simulating or duplicating the sexually abusive behavior of the adults in the family or assuming fully the parental roles in a family where the adults are failing to parent the children.

It has been our experience that sibling incest is not initiated or continued by mutual consent. Usually the oldest male child forces the cooperation or submission of younger siblings. The threat of physical violence or actual violence accompanies the incidents of sexual activity.

The social development of youngsters involved in sibling incest is detrimentally affected by the incest in that it limits or substitutes for heterosexual relationships with their peer group. It prevents them from learning how to establish and maintain intimate relationships with members of the opposite sex outside of their own family.

It is our belief that in families where sibling incest occurs, sex is the vehicle for the expression of love and nurturance. It occurs when parents do not meet their children's needs for love, affection, and nurturance.

## MEN IN A PARENTAL ROLE

A common characteristic we find in abusive men in a parental role is early loss and separation in the family of origin. The loss may involve physical separation from one or both parents or an emotionally unavailable parent. In other words, the picture is of a man who has experienced emotional deprivation at an early age. This man often has strongly ambivalent feelings toward his own father; he admires and respects his father as well as hates and fears him. Our clinical experience has been that a man in this group will first describe physically and emotionally abusive incidents in his early childhood and then refuse to acknowledge them as excessively harsh. After several months of intensive therapy, he may reveal that he too was sexually victimized as a child, usually by his father. He often describes being closer to his mother, although that relationship is frequently characterized as cold and distant.

This man has low self-esteem and lacks a sense of masculine identity. He attempts to compensate by projecting an image of role competence. In his current family, which is tightly controlled by intimidation, he appears to be the dominant member. He is possessive of his spouse and children, often isolating them from peers and the community. At the same time, he is apt to be extremely dependent on his family for emotional support. Although he is dominant in many situations and interactions, he is likely to be sexually passive with adult women. The family messages are: "We must take care of Daddy or he will fall apart" and "We must keep up the image that he is strong and in control, or we may fall apart or be hurt."

A man in this group has not had an opportunity to learn the special value of a parent-child relationship. He describes his children as one would describe an object. The child is seen as "just another kid," someone who is available to meet his needs for nurturance and support, or someone to do things for him.

Viewed from the outside, the family appears rather traditional and somewhat role-rigid, with the father as the "good provider." He may well have a good employment record, but the family is apt to be isolated. Moreover, the family has an intellectual defense structure and frequently engages in minimization, denial, and projection of blame. A man's first experience of molesting a child often happens when alcohol has lowered his inhibitions. The family will cling to the explanation that the alcohol made him do it, for it is incomprehensible that he would commit such an act under ordinary circumstances.

## THE FRIENDLY NEIGHBORHOOD MOLESTER

Pedophiles, or adults who molest children unrelated to them, usually have a history of sexual abuse and neglect in their own childhoods. Such adults' psychosocial development has been severely damaged by their experiences of abuse, as evidenced by their inability to establish or maintain trusting and intimate relationships with adults.

Pedophiles are terrified of intimacy with other adults. Relating intimately to children is nonthreatening because they feel fully in control of whatever happens. Pedophiles commonly learned early in life that adults could not be trusted to take care of them or to protect them.

Because pedophiles are severely maladapted psychosocially, they are not good candidates for diversion treatment programs. They should not be diverted into treatment in lieu of prosecution, nor should they be treated as outpatients while on probation. It is our experience that they can be most effectively treated in a totally controlled environment such as a prison mental hospital. They should not be treated together with adults who sexually abused their own children and fully acknowledge it; pedophiles' psychodynamics differ, and so should their treatment programs. It is clinically naive to offer the same treatment methods to both groups as if all adults who sexually abuse children are the same.

Studies of victimizers in this group divide them into two categories: those who are primarily sexually attracted to children and those who sexually molest children when under stress. Men in both groups seduce children by meeting the child's needs for attention, affection, and excitement. Lured by imagination, games, stories, secrets, affection, and material rewards, the child is seduced into cooperating. Pornography depicting adults and children engaged in sexual acts and pornography using familiar cartoon characters are frequently used to desensitize or sexually intrigue the children.

These men frequently find emotionally needy and unsupervised children who will participate in sexual acts often for months and sometimes for years. Coercion is seldom necessary, but as with the parent-role victimizer, if the child begins to resist, coercion, including threats of physical force, is used.

Men whose primary sexual interest is in children may also participate in adult sexual relationships, but the initiation generally comes from the partner. The adult sexual relationship is usually engaged in to disguise sexual preference. The choice of sex object appears to be the result of an arrested psychosocial development and is frequently focused on a particular age, sex, and type of child. Guilt, shame, and remorse are generally absent. If these feelings are expressed, they are related to the pedophile's having been discovered—not to the acts themselves.

These men experience their behavior as a compulsion. They are controlled by their needs and are not in command of their desires. Sometimes this compulsion can reach the level of an obsession, occupying their thoughts and affecting their behavior constantly. Functioning is generally marginal in many areas, and these men are easily overwhelmed by life's demands.

Other victimizers have developed mature forms of sexual relationships with adults and turn to a child as a sexual object when they are in conflict or under stress. These men have low self-esteem, and their feelings of inadequacy increase with a crisis that may be, for example, physical, social, vocational, marital, or financial. Power and sexual competence traditionally define a "real man" in the American culture. When a man in this group experiences a loss of power and sexual adequacy, he attempts to regain them in his sexual involvement with children, who are not usually able to reject, punish, or ridicule him. The act is impulsive and is usually committed when the man is depressed and simply doesn't care any longer about the consequences. After the act or acts, feelings of shame, guilt, and disgust are common.

## THE BOY NEXT DOOR

The psychosocial dynamics described for the adult pedophile are in the process of development in the adolescent sexual abuser. He too is frightened of relationships with peers and finds safety and a sense of control when relating to younger children.

A person's first sexually stimulating experiences make a strong impression on his or her psychosexual development; such incidents introduce specific stimuli that then become a part of a person's sexual repertoire. These stimuli are then sought out and reintroduced into future sexually stimulating situations. For the adolescent and adult pedophile, the child is the key stimulator. Relating sexually to children is the pedophile's way to gain mastery and control in sexual situations similar to those in which he had no control or mastery as a child, when *he* was the victim.

The defenses used by victim and victimizer—denial and minimization—are also used by the helping professions when confronted with adolescent sexual victimizers of small children. Policymakers in social agencies and juvenile court systems are sometimes reluctant to take the problem seriously. The first sexually abusive act reported to such authorities is often dismissed as an isolated incident or attributed to adolescent sexual experimentation. There is a concern that the adolescent victimizer will be stigmatized if help is offered through a social agency or through the courts. Thus these victimizers are often neither reported nor helped. Consequently, they seldom become part of the research studies that would validate the seriousness of the problem, encourage thorough reporting, and lead to the development of more treatment programs.

Where he is found in clinical experience and research studies, the boy-next-door victimizer is typically a nice young man—a quiet boy who keeps to himself, a loner. He is usually an average student who is often appreciated by educators because of his placating behavior. Notable characteristics are isolation from peers, low self-esteem, and a history of abuse, often sexual. Because he does not have friends who take up his time and because he is quiet and well behaved, he is often asked to babysit for small children. His victims are usually fond of him and will participate in sexual activities for long periods of time before the secret becomes too burdensome. When child victims attempt to describe what has happened to them, they are handicapped by their limited vocabulary, ignorance, shame, and fear. The children are frequently disbelieved because the adolescent babysitter, relative, or friend is known to the family and is "such a nice boy."

The victimizer as victim is seen most often among adolescent molesters. As with an adult victimizer, the boy rarely reveals his own physically or sexually abusive history until he has been in treatment long enough to develop some trust in his therapist. He is also reluctant to reveal any more about his sexually assaultive behavior than the therapist already knows. Often, after the secret is out, more child victims of the same offender will tell about their experiences. As their shame diminishes, or as they become assured that the adults around them can cope with the information, victims will reveal more about what happened.

Adolescent sexual assaults on young children appear to serve one or both of the following purposes in addition to sexual gratification: They may be an outlet to express hostility, a means to feel powerful, a way to master an event from the past, or a method of validating heterosexuality; or they may serve as an outlet to express hostility and to feel in control of situations.

An adolescent who molests younger children has learned that expressing hostility can be dangerous to himself and to his family. He inhibits and suppresses his aggressive impulses, channeling them into issues of power and control. He is unskilled and inexperienced socially and often feels helpless. Power and control are gained by sexually exploiting young children, who are accessible and are easily controlled by authority. Unlike parents or peers, small children are unable to retaliate.

A second cause of victimizing may be a need to master events in the molester's past. Some adolescents appear to repeat almost compulsively an act in their past that was psychologically traumatizing. This kind of victimization usually involves a male victim. The adolescent adopts the role of the aggressor and punishes the child for what he dislikes in himself—his weakness, his helplessness. By becoming the aggressor rather than the victim, he gains a sense of mastery. It is his defense against profound feelings of insecurity and vulnerability.

A third source of such behavior may be found in the adolescent's need for validating his heterosexuality. Many adolescent boys fear they are homosexual because of their own prior victimization by adult males. Because of their fears, their lack of social skills, and their own experience that children can be used, they assault young girls. We have worked with many cases in which the young male victim was molested by his father and, as part of this process, was required to participate in sex acts with his younger sister. The father often participated, coached, or masturbated on the sidelines. A young boy in these circumstances is not only used as a sex object by his father, he is required to victimize his younger sister; his most significant male role model has taught him how a male is to behave sexually in the world.

Will the adolescent repeat his pattern of molesting children if he is not treated? Will he become a neighborhood molester or an incestuous father? The answer to both questions is yes. Our clinical experience confirms this.

## WOMEN WHO SEXUALLY ABUSE CHILDREN

Describing and categorizing the sexual victimizers of children is an attempt to clarify what our own and others' experience has taught us. We sometimes feel like the seven blind men who tried to describe different parts of an elephant. There may be a large female elephant near us; we do not see her, but we sense that she is near.

The least reported incidents of molestation are those cases in which a female is the victimizer. Our information has been obtained from the victims of such abuse and not from women in treatment. Because in most cases the woman is in a maternal, caretaking role, she is referred to in this section as "mother."

Victims molested by mother seem to exhibit more confusion than other victims. These victims have many of the same conflicts as do girls who were victimized by males; that is, feelings of both love and hate toward the victimizer, self-loathing, a sense of responsibility for the acts, the feeling that they've betrayed a parent by telling, and so on. Although many child victims try to rationalize the parent's behavior, when the molester is a mother, the child's effort to make her behavior "acceptable" and to make her a "good" parent is profound. We believe that this confusion and the victims' denial of their abuse derive from the particular dynamics of the mother-child relationship.

First, the victim does not perceive the mother as a sexual person and has no information that relates in any way to the experience. Second, the sexual acts are disguised by the mother as normal caretaking activities, and the child is told that he or she has a dirty mind or is imagining things. Also, the mother is often the only adult in the child's life. It is too threatening for the child to believe that this parent is not a loving, caring person. Finally, victims know that they are being used sexually to gratify the parent, but if this is brought to anyone's attention, they fear that they will lose the parent, that they will not be believed, or that revealing the molestation will hurt the parent.

In the table below, we have illustrated a continuum of molestation behavior that ranges from eroticized verbal interactions to sexual intercourse. Because of the mother's traditional role as caretaker, she, more than a man, is able to hide the sexually exploitive nature of these activities from the child, from others, and, for a time, from herself. We also list some of the rationalizations mothers present to their children.

| Sexual Activity | Mother's Rationalizations |
| --- | --- |
| Erotic verbal interactions during the night, with intimate stroking | "You're the man in my life now."<br>"You're just like me when I was a little girl." |
| Intense body contact | "You're afraid (I'm afraid); so we can sleep together."<br>"This is good because you used to do this (fondle breast, snuggle) when you were a baby." |
| Genital manipulation and masturbation | "I'm just checking to be sure you're healthy."<br>"Let's compare our bodies."<br>"It's okay for you to hold my vibrator; it's just for health reasons." |
| Oral copulation | "This isn't really sex."<br>"I'm teaching you, gently." |
| Sexual intercourse | "I love you so much. No one else would understand our love." |

The psychological profile of these mothers is sketchy. However, we have found that they have these characteristics in common: infantile and extreme dependency needs; a spousal relationship that is absent or emotionally empty; extremely possessive and overprotective attitudes toward child victims; alcohol used as a crutch and as a disinhibitor to the expression of sexual feelings. Denial is used as a primary defense; such molesters expect their children to meet their emotional needs. Because of the mother's traditional role as caretaker, she is able to hide the sexually exploitive nature of these contacts.

Boy victims are usually in a role reversal with the absent father. The father is thought of and referred to as a child. The boy is the dominant male in the family in terms of decision making, meeting his mother's needs, and so on. He is simultaneously expected to behave as a young child and as an adult—to allow mother to bathe him, to sleep with him, and to examine his body for "health reasons."

Girl victims in such situations seem to be an extension of the mother. There is little if any recognition of the individuality of these children. The mother's sexual acts with the girl necessarily have a masturbatory quality.

As with other forms of sexual abuse of children, we are likely to find that increased reporting of these incidents will lead to a better understanding of the psychodynamics.

---

## Chapter Three

# Mothers of Incest Victims

The mother in an incestuous family is the cornerstone of effective intervention. Her ability to protect her children from the father's sexual assaults determines the length of time that incest continues. If children do not tell their mother of the incest or request her help in stopping it, it is usually because they do not perceive her as a person who is able to assume an assertively protective role. This is one example of the common role reversal between child victim and mother in incestuous families. The child is protecting the mother by not telling her of the incest and is, in essence, parenting the mother. In such cases, the child keeps the incest a secret, choosing to protect the mother's emotional or physical well-being instead of her own. When the child can no longer tolerate the abuse, she reports it to someone outside the family. The child literally sacrifices herself for the mother's sake.

Our clinical experience enables us to identify four main categories, or personality types, of mothers in incestuous families.

## THE PASSIVE CHILD-WOMAN MOTHER

The passive child-woman mother is extremely dependent and immature. She relies on her husband or other adults to make all decisions for her. Often she has not learned to drive a car or balance a checkbook. She relates to her oldest female child as a peer, confiding intimate matters and delegating many maternal responsibilities to her, such as housework and grocery shopping. This woman assumes an attitude of helplessness and seeming apathy to any form of conflict or problem situation. In relationships, she usually chooses authoritarian and abusive men. She embodies the victim role.

Mothers of incest victims often report inadequate parenting in their own childhoods. Passive child-woman mothers are likely to have been severely abused physically or emotionally deprived. Physical abuse is most often at the hands of the father. A significant number of these women report incest or molestation in childhood. Their relationships to their mothers are described as poor, and memories elicit feelings of anger and pain. The mothers are said to have been emotionally unavailable to them, sometimes physically unavailable as well. Mothers often modeled a victim role, tolerating abuse and degradation from their husbands. The children grew up assuming that abuse was part of what women had to live with. These women embody the term *learned helplessness*.

*Case Study*

## The Passive Child-Woman Mother: Karen

Karen is an obese thirty-two-year-old woman. She has a daughter, Gina, age six. Karen's husband, Ronald, age thirty-four, molested Gina for two years, from the time she was four until Gina reported the incest to her teacher. When the case was investigated, it was determined that Ronald had also molested numerous children in the neighborhood, all of whom were about the same age as Gina. Ronald was found to be a mentally disordered sex offender and is currently serving three years at Atascadero State Hospital.

Karen is the only daughter her parents had. As a child, she was ignored by her mother and physically abused by her father. When her mother died, Karen assumed the role of housekeeper for her father. Six months after Karen's mother's death, her father suffered a severe stroke that left him an invalid. Karen cared for him for six years until his death. She was twenty-five when he died. She met Ronald at a church function shortly after her father's death, and they married.

Karen reports that she and Ronald had sexual intercourse only until Gina was conceived. Their sexual activity usually consisted of Karen masturbating Ronald to ejaculation. She wondered why he was not more interested in sex, but they never discussed it.

Karen is Roman Catholic and very devout. She is quite active in her church, volunteering much time and many services. She is very dependent on her priest for advice and will not make any decision without his prior approval.

## THE INTELLIGENT, COMPETENT, DISTANT MOTHER

The intelligent, professionally competent, emotionally distant mother appears to be a model mother. She is intelligent and charming, runs her home efficiently, and verbally espouses the familiar American middle-class values. She knows exactly what to say and to whom to say it. Her intelligence allows her to manipulate professionals successfully with her sophisticated rationalization of the incest report. She resists relating to people on anything but an intellectual level; her logic serves to block interventions aimed at uncovering her role in the incest. She is charming and likable, and this seduces many professionals into rescuing her. She is usually married to a man who is not as well educated as she is but who is warm and nurturing.

The intelligent, competent, emotionally distant mother often describes her own mother as assertive, high achieving, competitive, and emotionally distant. She is likely to feel closer emotionally to her father than to her mother, especially if her father was the nurturer in the family of origin. She is often active in civic affairs and away from home quite a bit. Her husband is the children's caretaker and nurturer. Such a life-style, of course, affords the husband ample opportunity to molest the children.

Because the emotionally distant mother has associated males with nurturing, she often has more male than female friends. Sometimes her distrust of women may be expressed as open hostility. This type of woman may even treat her sons more warmly than she does her daughters.

*Case Study*

## The Intelligent, Competent, Distant Mother: Roberta

Roberta is a slim and attractive forty-year-old surgical nurse. She dresses with classic elegance. She has two children from her first marriage to a man she states she divorced when he turned into a "middle-aged hippie." Her second husband, Carl, age thirty-six, sells motorcycles. He is warm and somewhat bashful.

Carl molested Roberta's daughter, Lisa, age ten, for two years. From the time Lisa was eight, Carl would force her to masturbate him to ejaculation each evening after Roberta had gone to work. At the time, Roberta worked from 4:00 P.M. to 11:00 P.M. The molestation started when the family was living in San Francisco. When Lisa told Roberta of the molestation, Roberta told Carl to stop it. Because the incest continued, Lisa again complained to her mother. In an effort to make a new start, the family moved to Sacramento. However, this did not solve the problem; the molestation continued there, and Lisa ultimately reported it to her teacher.

Roberta's mother owned her own business and had long working hours. She is described as "emotionally cool." Roberta remembers her father as warm and loving. She recalls eating evening meals with her father and receiving lots of help with her homework. She recalls going to the movies with him and playing card games and Monopoly on weekends.

Material things mean a lot to both Roberta and Carl. When asked what they are most proud of, they respond, "Our beautiful home." They have a ten-room house with a pool in the most exclusive part of town.

## THE REJECTING, VINDICTIVE MOTHER

The rejecting, vindictive mother is openly hostile and threatening. She is also intelligent and resourceful. She will do anything to avoid admitting to herself that incest has occurred, even when her husband admits it to her face. This is why she is so dangerous to the child: she would rather have her children taken away from her than admit that the incest report is true. This type of mother disowns her child on learning of the incest. She may threaten never to speak again to the abused child, burn all the child's clothes, or give her things away. Such vindictiveness usually results in the child's retracting her report of the incest, and this is the intent of the mother's hurtful behavior. This woman is glad that her daughter assumed some of her responsibilities as wife and mother. She is usually a woman who openly expresses disgust with sex, considering it a wifely duty to be submitted to but never enjoyed. She is usually married to a passive, meek man who is more afraid of her than he is of jail.

The rejecting, vindictive mother usually has an aggressive and controlling mother with whom she may maintain a symbiotic relationship into adulthood. She was probably raised to view men as vehicles to respectable womanhood but not as life partners or emotional intimates. Her disdain for men is often thinly veiled. She tends to relate to women in a superficially warm manner, with an ever present smile maintained under strain. She is often accompanied by her mother to official appointments related to the incest, such as interviews with her husband's lawyer. She may insist on having no one else present when she visits her abused child at the children's shelter. She will attempt to prevent social workers, probation officers, and lawyers from seeing her husband unless she is present to control the interview. This type of mother makes it next to impossible to intervene effectively in the incest, because the children and the husband are so afraid of her rejection and wrath. The best way to protect children of mothers like this is to avoid returning them home until the treatment contract has been signed, although this is difficult, since these women are clever manipulators of people and systems.

*Case Study*

## The Rejecting, Vindictive Mother: Jayne

Jayne, age thirty-eight, is a woman of average height and build. She has been dyeing her hair for a number of years, and it has acquired a burned, strawlike appearance and texture from this treatment. She wears heavy makeup with very bright eye shadow and lipstick, giving the impression of a male in drag. She has a loud voice, which becomes louder when she is angry. When she is speaking to someone with power or authority, she lowers her voice almost to a whisper.

Jayne's husband, Dan, a car mechanic, is also thirty-eight years old. He is the same height as his wife but is quiet and soft-spoken. Dan molested their sixteen-year-old daughter, Julie, for ten years. He has admitted this to Jayne, but she does not believe him.

Jayne is a homemaker, just as her mother was when Jayne was growing up. Jayne's mother lives five blocks away from them now. Jayne remembers her mother as the strong parent. She has little respect for her father, whom she describes as a weakling who "never amounted to much of anything."

Jayne is proud of her children—the boys, that is. She complains that Julie has been trouble to her from the day she was born. She is quick to point out that Julie is a delinquent and a "lying little tramp."


## THE PSYCHOTIC OR SEVERELY RETARDED MOTHER

Psychotic mothers are unable to protect their children; their mental illness incapacitates them. Their effective functioning as mothers is severely limited by their illness. These women are more likely to participate actively in the molestation of their own children than are other types of mothers.

Psychotic mothers may be amenable to treatment, depending on their state of remission. If they are in remission, they are often quite receptive to treatment. The bulk of the treatment energy, however, should go into teaching the child of such a parent how to report and protect herself from future sexual assaults. If the child is too young and vulnerable to participate actively in her own future protection, the child should be placed outside the home until she is able to participate in her own protection or until the parent has learned more appropriate patterns of behavior for protecting her child.

A severely retarded mother with no awareness of the inappropriateness of incestuous behavior may condone and actively participate in the molestation of her own children. If she is unable to protect her children from sexual assaults or cannot learn not to molest them, she should not have care and custody of them. It is unrealistic and sadistic to place a child with such a parent, expecting self-protection until the age of majority.

The families with the greatest potential for change with therapy are families with either passive child-woman mothers or intelligent, competent, but emotionally distant mothers. The passive mothers respond well to a combination of:

1. Assertiveness training.
2. Reparenting techniques within ego-supportive individual therapy.
3. Reality therapy within a group experience for mothers of incest victims.

Competent but distant mothers respond best to a combination of:

1. Reparenting techniques within ego-supportive individual therapy.
2. Reality therapy within a group for mothers of incest victims.
3. At least six months of individual therapy, followed by couple or marital therapy focusing on communication.

It has been our experience that therapy on a weekly basis for a minimum of a year is necessary in order to replace the family's dysfunctional patterns with healthier, nonabusive ones.

*Chapter Four*

---

# The Cycle of Sexual Abuse

The sexual abuse of children can be considered a generational phenomenon. Therapists involved in treatment programs with abusive adults in such situations have documented that the abusers are very likely to have been abused themselves as children. At the same time, our clinical experience has also revealed that not all adults who have been sexually molested as children grow up to participate in the sexual abuse of their own or others' children. In this section, we will explore the generation-to-generation cycle of sexual abuse and consider methods of intervention that can, and many times will, successfully interrupt this dysfunctional behavior pattern.

Because the most socially disruptive molestation and abuse situations are intrafamilial, we will focus on families as a way of looking at the continuum. For simplicity's sake, we posit a situation that typifies the most common elements found in intrafamilial abuse situations with generational patterns.

## THE MARRIAGE

We arbitrarily select for our starting point the marriage, formal or common law, of two people, at least one of whom has been victimized sexually as a child. Each member of this partnership can be expected to share certain common attitudes and experiences: low levels of self-esteem, a fear of loss and separation, difficulty in trusting adults, and the belief that an intact family unit is preferable to separation or divorce. In many cases, two people who come together in a couple-bonding where child abuse is likely to occur were previously married, often at an early age, and then joined the new partner after a divorce (if the marriage was legal). Because of the failure of the earlier relationship, the couple is determined to make the new relationship work—no matter what.

The partners in this situation generally appear to be living a traditional family life. Each person is apt to be role-rigid in an attempt to appear role-competent. The man frequently possesses a stable employment record and engages in social activities that are socially defined as "male." The woman may or may not work outside the home; in either case, she views caring for home and family as her principal occupation and is usually considered "feminine" by others in the community. Outside the family, the man may appear to be the strong member of the union; however, the woman provides the emotional support for other family members and supports the man's feelings of competence.

Each partner in this situation brings to the relationship particular sexual attitudes and needs. When one or both have experienced sexual abuse as a child, they bring to the union sexual problems that may quickly be incorporated into a cycle of child sexual abuse. When the man has experienced early abuse, assertive or even aggressive behavior may be manifested outside the home. But in the family setting—and especially in his sexual behavior—he may be quite passive. His background might well include a cold or distant relationship with parents; his victimization as a child frequently leaves him with fears of homosexuality and feelings of sexual inadequacy as an adult.

A woman involved in abusive situations as a child may present the appearance of a model wife and mother but may actually find little pleasure in sexual encounters. As a child, she longed for and reached for closeness and nurturing and got a sexual response instead. As a woman, she may block herself from seeking affection and closeness with adults. If her mate is sexually passive, she may well greet his passivity with relief rather than concern. Male passivity may be seen as a sign of love, in that the male is not sexually demanding. In a group therapy session for couples who had been sexually victimized as children and whose own families were similarly marred, one woman reported:

> I dated Robert for a long time, and he didn't ask for sex. In fact, I felt so funny because he'd been spending all that money on dates. . . . I sort of asked him.

Another described a mutual disinterest in this way:

> Well, I was just tired of men who wanted it all the time. Jim and I slept together for a month before we had sex. He never said anything, but he knew I'd been molested as a child. I think he just wanted me to have time, you know.

Persons entering relationships as adults, with experiences of molestation as children, are often looking for someone to meet the pregenital needs that should have been met by their parents. Because they have not had these needs met, they do not trust adults, fear getting hurt, and do not know how to ask for what they need—experience has shown them that this is disappointing or dangerous. Therefore they do not know how to receive and do not have much to give.

## THE NEXT GENERATION

When two adults who were deprived of affection as children and whose avenues of gratification were closed by molestation situations have their own child, that child is perceived as a resource for meeting the parents' infantile needs. The parents entertain the magical belief that the child will give them the love, affection, tenderness, and caring they missed. They see the infant as a person who can be trusted. A baby will not ridicule, exploit, betray, or abandon them. A child increases their feelings of self-esteem and enhances their appearance of role-competence.

In many cases of child molestation, the family is emotionally isolated, although not necessarily physically isolated. Neither of the partners is likely to have the social skills or self-esteem to seek, obtain, or maintain relationships outside the family. Having grown to maturity in an isolated family, they repeat the experiences they have known.

In many sexually abusive families, there is a history of loss or separation from the family of origin. This loss underlies the parents' beliefs and increases their fears. Loyalty to the nuclear family means survival, and outsiders are viewed with distrust. The child in such a family learns this lesson well.

## Toddlers

The mother in a potentially abusive system begins to withdraw physically from the child when it becomes a toddler. She is uncomfortable with touching the child after infancy, for touching is associated with sexuality. The following are typical comments from mothers of molested children who were themselves molested as children. These statements were made during group therapy with the authors.

> I've heard about that [that it's good for children to be cuddled], but I just can't do it. I mean Davy's only three and he . . . well . . . he, he put his head right on my breast when I put my arm around him watching TV.
>
> What does that mean to you?
>
> Well, you know. [Blushing] He wanted . . . he was trying to get a feel.
>
> I know what you mean. My daughter's little and she'll try to look at my . . . well, my pubic hair. I have to be careful.
>
> These kids will climb all over you and try things. Joanne [age 4] is always trying to get on my husband's lap.
>
> My son's only two and a half. I saw him with an erection when he was looking at pictures in *Playboy*.

The mothers speaking above had, as children, sought affection from adults and had received instead sexual exploitation. The children's demands for loving and cuddling are filtered through the mothers' childhood experiences, which have taught them that affection and sexual experiences are the same. The children's behavior is interpreted as sexual, and the mothers are likely to be frightened of their emotional response to their children. Because this early period of development represents the time when their own mothers withdrew from them, they may expect their children to begin to parent them and to meet some of their emotional needs. Thus role reversal in molestation situations may begin quite early.

At this point, sexual activity within the marriage relationship may diminish significantly. As the wife feels more entrenched in the marriage, she is able to withdraw from what she has been unable to enjoy. Her experience from childhood has been that sex is intense, powerful, and exploitive and leaves one vulnerable. The husband in such a situation feels less manly because of his wife's sexual withdrawal and silently blames her. He is angry, hurt, and in many cases desensitized to exploiting a child, for he may himself have been so exploited. The father, like the mother, may also have learned to turn to the child for tenderness and companionship.

It is the child-wife who rushes up to the husband when he gets home to ask how his day has been. It is the child-mother who comforts her own mother when the latter is in distress and needs to talk about her problems. The father, who has enmeshed affection with sexuality, becomes seductive with the child as the mother grows distant.

A variation of the motivational factors precipitating the onset of molestation is the father's experience of childhood abuse by a woman whom he knew as his mother or mother-surrogate. Such molestation experiences create much emotional conflict in the boy. He is angry for having been betrayed or abused; he feels guilty for having responded; he is frightened and frustrated by his inability to stop the situation. A boy frequently copes with this confusion of feelings in the following ways:

1. He may choose to relate sexually only to women his mother's age to make the experience feel less unusual.
2. He may be able to function sexually only when the female partner is helpless—that is, he may become a rapist.
3. He may be able to function sexually only with females who are different from his mother in looks and age—that is, he may become a pedophile.
4. He may choose homosexuality as a defense against sexual feelings for a mother figure.

When the wife becomes a mother, she also becomes the mother to the man. Although this awareness may remain on an unconscious level, it is often expressed as a change in the marital relationship coinciding with the birth of the first child. The man's conflicting childhood feelings about his mother emerge, and molestation may be one way of coping with these conflicts.

## Preschoolers

Sexual exploitation of a child often begins when the child is four or five years old—an age when children love adult attention, games, and secrets. They are easily seduced by someone whom they have learned to trust and to look to for guidance. Oral copulation, masturbation, and genital manipulation are presented as love, fun, or their secret. The child often experiences bodily pleasure as well as feelings of power. The child and one parent share a secret and a special relationship that they hide from the other parent. The child becomes "special" and is treated differently by the father. If the specialness is negative, she will try harder to please him. If the specialness is positive, it often elicits resentment from others in the family, and the child experiences alienation from them. Because of this, she clings to her father even more and tries even harder to please him.

The roles and alliances within the family become more confused. The father is the authority with power, and he is also the child's lover. The child has some power as a lover but must obey as a child. The child is the mother's confidant, responsible for her emotional well-being, but must act as though the mother is in charge. The child is alienated from siblings because of the special relationship with the parent. All must appear role-competent to the outside world.

## School-Age Children

The school-age child begins to learn from peers that sex is something secretive to giggle about nervously, that sex with a parent does not happen to other children, and that it is "nasty." The child's behavior is influenced and changed by her different developmental stages. For example, the secret and the special relationship in the family lose their power, and the child desires affinity with peers as she matures. As she is pulled toward her peers, her isolation is more strongly enforced by her parents because of the father's fear of disclosure. As the child resists the parent's sexual overtures, more extreme forms of coercion are used. Money, toys, and special privileges are often awarded. Suggestions are made that the mother would be devastated if she found out, that the father would be punished, or that everyone in school would find out. And, appealing to her belief that it is her responsibility to maintain the family, the father tells her that he will not molest the younger children in the family if she continues to cooperate.

The child's isolation and feelings of shame increase. She is socially unskilled and awkward with peers. At times, she believes that others can just look at her and know what she has been doing. Resentment toward her mother builds. Since she is parenting her mother, she cannot turn to her for emotional support; in fact, she believes she must protect her mother from knowing. And yet, since mothers are supposed to know everything, it seems to the child that her mother probably does know and is not doing anything to stop it. The child will often leave evidence so that her mother will find out. For example, the child may pull back the covers when there is a blood stain on the sheet, or she may leave panties with sperm in them in a corner of the living room. The child's anger increases with her attempts to seek protection. The multiple pressures on the child often affect her schoolwork. All of the conflicting messages she receives leave her confused. As an adult, she will probably experience confusion and feelings of helplessness when under stress— the same feelings her own mother may experience as she begins to pick up clues about what is happening in the family.

The child often symbolically tries to let others in her life know what she is experiencing. This may surface in play, in drawings, or in sexual acting-out behavior. For example:

- Johnny was caught trying to insert one of his toys in the rectum of the family dog.
- Sandy went to school without panties and displayed herself to the boys in the schoolyard.
- Lisa cut holes in the crotch of her dolls.

After discovering the sexually abusive behavior, the mothers acknowledge that the signs were obvious. They feel guilty about not having drawn conclusions from the evidence. In retrospect, it is easy to see; however, these women were blocked from knowing because of their own fears. They cannot believe the horror is happening again to their child. They are frightened to think that their spouse could prefer the child as a sexual partner. The mothers sometimes know about the molestation and feel helpless and confused. More subtly, they sometimes feel that because no one could stop the behavior when they were children, no one can stop it now.

In a family situation such as this, the system of communication is vague and talk of sexuality is almost nonexistent. Children from these families often have no names for genitalia, which is another block to telling anyone what is happening. The little knowledge they have gained from school and peers increases their fears. The girl sometimes worries that she is pregnant, even though menarche is years away and the sexual activity is oral; the boy is sure he is "queer."

In these situations, the child assumes responsibility for her own victimization. She has learned that it is her responsibility to keep the family together. If she has experienced orgasm during sexual acts with the parent, she may feel especially guilty; she may believe that because it takes two, like fighting, she should have stopped it. When the parent reinforces this by telling the child that she wants it and likes it, the child believes it. The shame then escalates, and the child's self-esteem lowers.

## Adolescents

Adolescent needs for peer relationships, for a sexual identity, and for separation from parents exacerbate the problems in the sexually abusive family. The adolescent becomes more aware of her exploitation by the parent. The repertoire of sexual behavior usually includes intercourse by now, and this increases the pressure on the child. At this point, the offending parent may begin to use threats of violence to perpetuate and contain the situation. Self-blame and the feeling that she must protect the family are still there for the adolescent, but anger toward the parent grows. Indeed, shame increases as well if the adolescent has been accepting bribes or extorting favors.

## DISCLOSURE

The factor that triggers a revelation of the sexual behavior is usually related to a power struggle between the exploitive parent and the adolescent. The parent behaves like a jealous lover and becomes increasingly fearful of disclosure. The parent will not allow the child to date, to attend a special school function, or to spend the night with a friend. The adolescent at this point tries to escape from family controls, often by running away. Because the child is so isolated and is not "street wise," she is usually caught and is then terrified of returning home. The child wants the behavior to stop, but the family must be protected, and feelings of shame and responsibility are great. Usually, the girl deals with this by telling the authorities that her father has made sexual overtures or that they had sex with each other once or twice—when the parent was drinking, she hastens to add.

A boy usually will not tell of the sexual exploitation; his sense of shame and confusion is perhaps even greater. He is treated as a delinquent. Sometimes the boy is caught in the trap of having identified with his aggressor and is himself discovered molesting a younger child. Knowledge that a boy has been sexually molested usually comes from another person who discovers the child and parent in the act or finds pictures. The victims minimize and deny the sexual abuse to save their families and to save themselves. It is important to remember that the child's ambivalent feelings toward the offending parent are both hateful and loving. The parent has not only exploited the child but also nurtured him.

### The Parents' Reactions

The parents are confronted with this initial information by the authorities. In private, the molesting parent will admit to his partner that he approached the child once or twice because the child was so seductive and wanted the parent—obviously this is true because the child did not tell anyone when it happened. Sometimes, the molesting parent will state that although the act might have occurred, he cannot remember it because he was drunk. His overwhelming fear of the possible consequences is interpreted as remorse. The parent may swear that it will never happen again; he will make it up to the family—promise anything—but he cannot prove it if he is in jail, or if he loses his job, or if the family is separated.

In instances involving girls and their fathers, the mother may initially support her daughter, but many times the mother changes her attitude in a few weeks. The mother fears living without her spouse. She is sure she cannot make it on her own, and she is sure he will not make it either. She wants so badly to believe her husband that she begins to minimize and deny the sexual abuse. She begins to focus on the child's "seductive" behavior in the past, the child's "special" treatment, and her chafing under the limits set by the father. The mother may be convinced that the girl seduced the father or that she lied to get even because she was not allowed to date. The mother will suggest that the girl change her story to the authorities. She may tell her that her father has admitted the indiscretion and has promised that it will never happen again. The mother may simply act very depressed and talk of all the terrible consequences: losing income, losing the home, giving grandparents heart attacks, and shaming the family. The emotional pull for the girl to take care of her mother is very strong.

## The Child's Reactions

In molestation situations like these, the adolescent is questioned in the police station and is brought to a children's shelter or placed in a foster home in most social service and enforcement systems. The child is alone, frightened, and apt to feel that she deserves what is happening to her, since she let the family down. She believes that all of this is happening because she told, not because of what the parent did. The victim wants it all to go away and will often change the story to fit the parent's account of the situation. The myth that angry adolescents will lie about being molested is thus reinforced in all professionals who have had contact with them and who do not understand the child's ambivalence, fears, and feelings of responsibility toward the family. A changed story usually returns the victim to her home. The molestation will probably continue, and the victim will feel even more helpless, for who will believe her now?

If the child does not change the story, she assumes responsibility for all the negative consequences that affect the family. All negative statements made about the offending parent are taken to mean her as well. Guilt increases, as does depression, although it too will be masked, along with most feelings. These pseudomature adolescents have learned to hide their feelings, keep secrets, and know what adults need to hear. They do well in psychiatric evaluations when the professional is unfamiliar with the dynamics of sexually abusive families, as illustrated in the following cases:

> Larry, age sixteen, had been sodomized and forced to orally copulate with his father since he was seven years old. He was being evaluated by a psychiatrist because both he and his father were charged with molesting his younger sister. The psychiatrist stated that Larry should not be held responsible because he was himself a victim and had been

coerced by his father to have sex with the little girl. He further stated that psychotherapy was not needed for Larry because he was coping well. The reports by a psychologist suggested that possibly a therapeutic session or two might be useful for Larry to sort out what had happened to him.

Nancy, age fourteen, had two children by her father. She was placed in one foster home and the children in another. She was quiet and cooperative, and she visited the children and her family regularly. When it was suggested to the social worker that Nancy get some psychological help, she stated that Nancy was doing just fine. She did not think that Nancy should have to relive in therapy what had happened to her but should just forget about it.

The adolescents' confused sexual identity, feelings of shame, and low self-esteem lead them to partners who generally feel the same. On the outside they look good—role-competent. And they want so desperately to have a family that they marry, often starting the cycle again.

# Part Two

---

# Family Treatment

Part 2 contains the kind of information on treatment that we searched the literature in vain for when we began to work with sexually abusive families. We hope that therapists will find it useful to read our definitions of what qualities are essential for them to work effectively with these families. Self-examination is a necessary growth process for therapists, and we believe an honest self-appraisal at the outset will help prepare therapists for their difficult task. The rewards of doing treatment with sexually abusive families are slow in coming. The therapist needs to be highly self-motivated and to have a good support base to do this work.

This section of the book will also describe the phases of treatment and treatment exercises recommended for use in each phase. Critical family sessions are described in detail, and their role in the treatment process is identified and discussed.

A clear understanding of the clinical basis for our treatment philosophy is essential for a full appreciation of the concepts described and the methods recommended. We believe that child sexual abuse can be most effectively dealt with using a family systems model. The sexual abuse is viewed as one of a number of symptoms of family dysfunction. It is the vehicle carrying the message that the family is functioning as a closed family system. For a full discussion of the open versus closed family systems model, see the writings of Virginia Satir, Martin Kirschenbaum, Shirley Luthman, Salvador Minuchin, Murray Bowen, and Jay Haley.

The family systems model of treatment does not necessarily involve the whole family in treatment. It can be used effectively with individual, couple, group, or conjoint family therapy. What the family systems approach does is acknowledge that the dyads, alliances, and contracts in a family affect each family member's functioning. Individuals' functioning is viewed in terms of the survival choices they have made, behaviorally and attitudinally, in order to get their needs met.

Other treatment models incorporate peer group therapy or self-help groups into their therapy program. We believe that the self-help component, such as the Parents United Groups pioneered by the Santa Clara County Child Sexual Abuse Treatment Program, is a valuable component of the treatment process. There is no substitute for the support of someone who has experienced life in a sexually abusive family. Such groups should be an adjunct to therapy guided by an experienced clinician within a program centered on the protection of the child victim.

With the family systems model, it takes a minimum of one year of intensive treatment for family members to gain insight into themselves and the others in their family. Attitude changes occur gradually over time in both the victimizers and the victims. The sexual abuse cannot be allowed to continue while these attitude changes are occurring. The only effective way to put an immediate stop to the sexual abuse is to use the power of the courts. Therapy for the treatment of child sexual abuse is not effective without this authority. As mentioned earlier, it is our belief that it is essential to use the power of the courts to maintain the family in treatment for the extended period of time necessary for changes to occur.

The traditional protective services model, which may use the power of the juvenile court to order the family into treatment, is ineffective with sexually abusive families because the juvenile court does not have a degree of power equal to that of the District Attorney's office. Additionally, when the juvenile court orders families into treatment, the therapists are not usually connected to the child welfare system. Therapists in private practice are commonly hesitant and uncomfortable using the power of the courts to protect the child. Private therapists do not commonly do outreach when clients drop out of therapy, nor do they function primarily as child advocates. For these reasons therapists in private practice who treat sexually abusive families should establish a working relationship with the various available resources in the child welfare and legal systems.

The effective treatment of pedophiles (adults who sexually abuse children unrelated to them by blood or marriage) is different from that of sexually abusive parents. Rehabilitation of the pedophile is discussed in Chapter 2. Children who have been sexually abused by an unrelated adult should be referred for individual or play therapy in the private-practice community. They can also benefit from one-to-one contact with another victim of similar age and maturity. It is helpful for these children to know they are not the only ones who have been sexually abused. However, they should not be placed in a group with children sexually abused by parents.

The role of concurrent therapies (group, individual, couple, and conjoint) will be discussed in Part 2 from the perspective of goal attainment in each phase of treatment. This part includes a detailed description of numerous treatment exercises that experienced therapists can creatively modify to support the treatment plan for their client. We invite therapists to communicate to us their experiences with these exercises.

## Chapter Five

# *The Therapists*

## PERSONAL QUALITIES AND CLINICAL SKILLS

In general, therapists must be comfortable with being both authoritative and warm; they must have clear standards regarding sexual abuse; and they must be comfortable communicating openly, honestly, and clearly. A permissive attitude is not consistent with the therapeutic needs of clients from sexually abusive families. It is essential that therapists feel comfortable with all aspects of human sexuality so that they can facilitate discussions of sexually abusive experiences and their client's feelings about those experiences.

Therapists should be skilled in the use of a variety of therapeutic techniques and open to the use of techniques extracted from a variety of current psychotherapies, including Gestalt therapy, reality therapy, and conjoint family therapy.

The characteristics that are absolutely essential to this work are:

1. Comfort in relating to a co-therapist of the opposite sex as an equal. This quality is necessary for the team to model male-female equality in relationships and other facets of human living.
2. Comfort in dealing with and expressing feelings of pain, helplessness, fear, vulnerability, and grief. Again, this quality is necessary for role modeling. If group leaders are uncomfortable expressing vulnerability, clients will be unable to express *their* vulnerability.

3. Comfort and ease with personal sexuality and with open discussions of any and all issues relating to human sexuality. One of the things clients say helps them talk about sex and sexual abuse is that the therapists "desensitize" them by openly talking about these things.

4. The ability to communicate in an open, honest, warm, and nurturing manner and to recognize and to comment on the co-therapist's attitudes and moods. For example, one therapist may note to the group that his female co-therapist looks tired and ask her if that is so. She validates his observation. He asks her if she would like her shoulders massaged, and if she thinks that would make her feel better. She says she would like a shoulder massage. He gets up from his chair and stands behind her chair, massaging her shoulders while explaining to the group that there is nothing sexual about the massage. He explains that he and the co-therapist are friends and that this is one way that friends can be nurturing to one another. It is not uncommon that "permission in action" relieves anxiety about certain forms of relating, and an invitation to participate in a like manner is accepted by most group members.

5. Comfort in being assertive, vocally intense, and confrontive. Therapists must be able to assume power and control when necessary. Abused children and adults abused as children have often been related to by parents at a high level of vocal intensity. That is, they have been yelled at or screamed at on a regular basis, often just prior to being physically abused. It is therefore sometimes necessary to yell or speak very loudly to get such a client's attention or to help an idea sink in. When the therapist has gotten the client's attention, she then makes the positive communication in a normal tone of voice. This rather unconventional technique takes getting used to, but it is quite effective.

6. Comfort in relating in an emotionally intimate manner to the co-therapist and the willingness to contract with the co-therapist not to be sexually intimate while co-leading the group. Working with abused children and their families is very intense, emotionally exhausting, and challenging work. It is natural for a male-female co-therapy team to develop a close and caring relationship over time, especially since in many ways they are

relating to one another as a couple in a group as they model relationships and communication for clients. Emotional intimacy between the co-therapists should not include sexual intimacy, because this will contaminate their work together.

Child clients need the fantasy, usually formed, that their co-therapists are truly intimate, since they see them as parent-surrogates. The group leaders should not try to convince the child that such a fantasy is unrealistic or unnecessary. Instead, the children should be encouraged to talk about what a marriage between the co-therapists would be like and what characteristics in the co-therapy relationship remind them of qualities in a good marital relationship. The exploration of this theme in treatment is very important and valuable, and for the therapists to become entangled in the content would prevent positive exploration of this topic.

7. Therapists need a good sense of humor. Children can deal effectively with sensitive topics, especially when there is humor involved. Resistance can also be confronted effectively with humor. Humor is also effective in relieving the tension in a group following discussion of an intense topic.

*Chapter Six*

---

# Phases of Treatment

Therapeutic help for the family in which sexual abuse has occurred deals with interpsychic and dyadic issues, but within a family system's interactional framework. The functioning of the family—its roles, alliances, power, communication, conflicts, and so on—is the focus of treatment, whether the therapist is seeing a family member individually, with another person, or in a group setting. The table on page 54 lists the phases of treatment, the therapeutic modality for each phase, and the critical family sessions required for the child's protection in each phase. Clinicians will use all or part of these therapies, depending on the family's needs and the resources available in the community.

### DISCLOSURE-PANIC PHASE

The disclosure-panic phase brings the family into contact with a number of professionals whose primary objectives vary. It is important that clinicians clearly and frequently state their role to the family. For example, that role might be one of advocate for the child, with the goal of helping the family get through the legal process or assisting them in therapy without further trauma to the child. It is important to take the firm stance that incestuous behavior is unacceptable while at the same time acknowledging the fears and concerns of the family members. This is the most critical and burdensome time for the therapist, who must handle the family's anger, denial, projection, intellectualizing, and attempts to refocus the problem elsewhere—often on the therapist. This calls on the greatest skills of the clinician: to be supportive and to

### Phases of Treatment

| Phase | Duration | Therapeutic Modality | Critical Family Sessions |
|---|---|---|---|
| Disclosure-panic phase | 2 weeks to 3 months | Individual crisis therapy with all group members | |
| | | Peer group support | |
| Assessment-awareness phase | 6 months to 1½ years | Individual therapy: mother, father, child victim | Confrontation |
| | | Peer group therapy | Defining the abuse pattern |
| | | Mother-child therapy | Outlining goals |
| | | Couples group therapy (if goal is reunification) | Establishing visitation plan |
| | | Father-child therapy | Discussion of progress |
| Restructure phase | 1½ to 2 years | Conjoint family therapy | Adjustment after reunification |
| | | Outreach to others via peer group | Termination of treatment |

communicate clearly with the family, to stay focused on the issues, and to demonstrate both firmness and caring for the family members. This is the foundation for all treatment to follow.

The use of crisis therapy techniques when working individually with parents is helpful during this phase. These family systems are tightly closed and the communication style is vague and secretive. The crisis is an opportunity to open the system and helps break through the denial process.

The parents may rage, act out violently, and state, for example, that the child is an angry, lying slut or that they have been betrayed. At the other end of the spectrum are parents who make statements like: "I don't remember, but if I did do such a horrible thing, I should be locked up forever." The denial is strong, as are the conflicts and the feelings of guilt and shame. These parents are in crisis. This is not the time for the therapist to reflect feelings or to probe for insights. This is the time to take a firm stand, to protect and to guide all of the members of the family. The therapist must assess and deal with the potential for suicide and other self-destructive behaviors. The resources and options available to the family must be examined and their strengths recognized.

The clinician can often help the family by telling them in advance what to expect from the legal and social service systems and what emotional reactions are likely to occur. The parents' greatest concerns at this point are loss and separation. Indeed, sexual abuse within the family can be a defense against loss and separation. This fear can be used to mobilize the family. When met with blasts of denial, rage, and projection, the therapist can avoid responding to these while reaching for deeper feelings and constantly reassuring the family that others have weathered this kind of crisis successfully.

Though many women initially support their children, often within a week or two they reverse their positions and protect the fathers. The mothers appear to believe that these men would not lie to them about anything so important, or they believe that the men will be able to follow through with their promises that the sexually abusive behavior will not continue. The mothers need to believe this because they often feel that their lives will be destroyed if they do not protect the men. A woman in this situation is in a double bind and believes that she loses regardless of the decision she makes. The clinician can focus on the double bind and help the mother explore her feelings of being trapped and frightened.

When dealing with the child, the therapist must constantly tell her that her report of molestation is believed. Often the child victim, overwhelmed by the parents' denial and the chaos created by the disclosure, will change her story and deny the abuse. Therapists may question whether a child will confide in them and whether the child will tell the truth. It has been our experience that children will tell people what they believe those people can cope with emotionally. These children have been socialized to meet the needs of adults and quickly assess what is "safe" to tell. For example:

Six-year-old Ellen told her mother that Daddy bothered her, told her teacher that Daddy played with her and she didn't like it, told her friend that Daddy showed her his pee-pee, and told a well-trained juvenile officer that Daddy put his pee-pee in her mouth and sticky stuff came out of it.

A clinician will have little doubt of sexually abusive behavior when very young children describe ejaculation, erection, oral copulation, and attempted anal and vaginal penetration. With older victims the affect is often extreme anger, shame, or fear—all overlaid with a protective concern for the parents and an acceptance of the responsibility themselves. The children say, "Make it [the behavior] stop, but don't make waves. I don't think they [the parents] can take it." Unfortunately, there are people in the child's life who will doubt the reported story and question its validity in subtle and not-so-subtle ways. As a survival mechanism, abused children have learned to be quite sensitive to verbal and nonverbal cues. They quickly grasp the meaning behind such questions as: "Do you know what *homosexual* means?" "Did you enjoy it?" "You were really angry when your father restricted you from seeing your friend. How close are you and your friend?"

Several writers have pointed out that child victims are further traumatized by sudden, temporary removal from their homes. That point cannot be argued. However, children in therapy have expressed their rage and deep sense of betrayal when they remain in the home and are exposed to their parents' denial, anger, nonsupport, and pressure to change their stories. Many sexually abused children in therapy report that they told the police and others that they had lied about the sexual abuse. They changed their story to protect their parents and also because they believed their parents' promises that it would not happen again. These children were returned to their homes, and the sexual abuse continued. The children were then certain that no one would believe them again if they told about the sexual activity. A younger child believed that the police would punish her if she reported again because she once lied to them.

Individual supportive therapy is used to reassure the children throughout the myriad environmental changes that they are undergoing during the disclosure-panic phase. Peer counseling can be very helpful, as can group therapy with other children who have been exposed to sexual molestation in their families. This dispels the victim's belief that no one else has ever experienced this type of abuse and the feelings that reporting the abuse is betraying the family.

| | Disclosure-Panic Phase | |
| --- | --- | --- |
| Family Member | Behavior | Underlying Feeling |
| Father | *Denial of incest* | I will lose my job; my wife will leave me. |
| | *Anger toward victim or violent acting out* | Because of her I'll be arrested and put in jail. |
| | | That child had no right to tell anyone; after all, I'm the father. |
| | *Self-destructive acts or withdrawal* | Everyone will know and no one will understand. |
| Mother | *Anger toward offender* | How could he do this to me? |
| | *Fear of consequences* | I will lose my home, my income, and my man. |
| | | I must choose between him and my child. |
| | *Shame* | I'm not much of a woman if he prefers having sex with an immature child. |
| | | What will people say? |
| | | I must be a bad parent, or I would have known about this sooner. |
| | *Denial of incest* | I know he won't do it again; I must keep the family together. |
| | *Anger toward victim* | Maybe some of those things did happen, but surely everyone knows how children's imaginations are and how they misinterpret things. |
| Child victim | *Guilt* | I only wanted it to stop; now I've caused all this trouble. |
| | *Self-blame* | If only I hadn't sat on his lap, been in just my underwear, and so on. |
| | *Fear* | Mom believes him and not me. |
| | *Shame or depression* | I know I've done wrong and deserve to be punished like this (by police, courts, foster care, and so on). |
| Siblings | *Fear* | What will happen to me and the family? |
| | *Anger toward victim* | My mom and dad wouldn't lie. |
| | *Internal confusion* | I can't tell what I know and betray the family. |

## ASSESSMENT-AWARENESS PHASE

The assessment-awareness phase of treatment is characterized by dependency on the therapist, eagerness for insights into self, lowering of defenses, and a degree of excitement about the newly discovered potential for personal growth that resembles religious fervor. It is a demanding phase for therapists because it requires much energy, patience, and insight. A variety of skills are necessary for the therapist to be effective in helping the family through this difficult phase. Although the parents no longer deny that the abuse occurred, many of them still blame the victim, however subtly, or they blame alcohol or extenuating circumstances.

The crisis of disclosure is over, and the panic brought on by threatened survival is past. The possibilities for a "new life" are both exciting and frightening for the parents. Although the relationship the family has had thus far has been unfulfilling and disappointing, there has been safety in familiarity and in the absence of risk. The prospect of more rewarding relationships is appealing but terrifying. Thus, ongoing contact in a group setting with other couples who are struggling to open up their relationships is the best source of support and encouragement for couples who want to change.

Seven critical family sessions are required in treatment. They are specifically designed to prevent further molestation. These sessions are concurrent with ongoing therapies and may include nonfamily members such as a probation officer or social worker. The sessions are described in detail in Chapter 7.

Early in this phase of treatment, or when the child feels ready, there must be a family confrontation session where the sexual abuse is discussed openly for the first time. This allows the victim to express her feelings in a safe environment. It forces the molesting parent to face the true effects of the behavior on the child. The confrontation brings to the attention of the other children in the family the feelings and fears of their sibling and thereby removes much of their risk of molestation. It is during this session that the family wanting to reunite makes a commitment to change and to work together toward preventing further sexual abuse. This family session is advised even when the parents have decided to separate or divorce, because the primary goal of such a session is to provide the family with a safe arena in which to express their true feelings about the sexual abuse. This is a meeting in which all family members are beginning to learn to communicate openly.

A second family session to define the abuse pattern is held two to four weeks after the confrontation session. The goals are to let everyone understand how and when the molestation occurred in the past. This session requires that the nonmolesting parent examine her role in the abuse. Family members learn the pattern unique to their family and learn to recognize the signs so that they can take steps to prevent its recurrence. The symbolic value of this family session lies in the fact that the family declares sexual abuse a part of their past family history and banishes it from their future family system. In this sense, the old family dies, and the new family, yet to be designed and constructed, is born.

It is during this phase of treatment, when families feel exhilarated by their growth, that they feel the impulsive urge to share their sexual abuse problem with others. It is extremely important for therapists actively to protect such families, who often do not consider the risk of disclosure. Protecting the family members from themselves takes a significant percentage of time during this phase. The therapist needs to remind the family that most of the world still considers incest and molestation taboo and that admitting such a problem to such people is sure to bring on rejection, alienation, and perhaps ridicule.

After the legal aspects of the molestation charges have been resolved, family members can think clearly about their alternatives and make decisions about the future of the family. A family session for outlining goals is needed at this time. Although the family may have informally discussed their plans, the ritual and process of making choices together is a valuable learning experience. The development of short-term and long-term goals helps the family to focus on the work that needs to be accomplished and to feel a sense of achievement when a goal has been reached.

During the assessment-awareness phase of treatment, marital therapy and couples group therapy is essential for those families that plan to remain together. Reality therapy and experiential techniques help to bypass much of the couple's rationalizing and many of their attempts to manipulate. A phenomenon of instant insight will sometimes occur at this time, when the person in therapy attempts to avoid the painful exploration of past and present behavior by labeling one thing as the cause of the sexual abuse.

They proceed to deal with the identified cause—they find God, stop drinking, get a job, lose weight, and so on—and then pronounce themselves cured. In a couples group the members confront this kind of behavior. They also support one another, feel less isolated, and identify with each other's successes.

The focus of treatment in couples' groups is on open communication, exploring marital dysfunctions, identifying interpsychic conflicts, and discerning how these dysfunctions and conflicts may have contributed to the incestuous behavior. The couple also learns, through assertiveness training, to express their needs and to negotiate conflicts.

Both in individual treatment and in group work, therapists will find that parents often become depressed as they become more aware of the pain experienced by themselves, by their partner, and by their children. They do not want the sexually abusive behavior to happen again but are secretly afraid that it will. They are not certain that they will be able to prevent it or stop it. All family members must be continually supported in the growth they have accomplished. They must meet others who have successfully been through treatment, and, most importantly, they must have hope. They need to learn that this painful treatment leads to an understanding of how the process started and how it was perpetuated and that this same treatment will help them change and prevent its recurrence.

For couples who decide to separate, individual therapy—concurrently with peer group therapy with other men or women who choose to separate from their partners—is most useful. In addition to dealing with their responsibility for and feelings about the sexual abuse, these people will be coping with the process of separation.

Midway through the assessment-awareness phase, mother-child therapy helps to establish a supportive relationship and to clarify role confusion in this relationship. Children often feel considerably more anger toward their mothers as the nonoffending parent than they do toward the offender. This is related to their belief that somehow their mothers should have been able to protect them; if their mothers had provided sexual enjoyment for their fathers, the children would not have had to fill in. At a deeper level, most children experience a sense of loss of the nurturing they needed from their mothers. The children are usually frightened of these feelings and are unable to express them. In many cases, they are already separated from their fathers and believe that they will somehow lose their mothers if they express their angry feelings.

The mothers also experience conflicting feelings. Many of them yearn for closeness with their daughters, but they are blocked from expressing or experiencing this because of these conflicts. They feel awkward and uncomfortable relating to what they now perceive as a child-woman who has experienced adult sexuality. They sometimes think of the child as the "other woman," and then powerful feelings of guilt and shame emerge for having had these feelings. There is also an overwhelming sense of having failed the child and not deserving her love and affection.

It is essential to the mother and child's continued growth in treatment that there be some reduction in these conflicted feelings and that the mother-child bond be strengthened. If the family's plan is reunification, a positive, strong mother-child relationship will give each of them the solid base needed to restructure their respective relationships with the formerly abusive parent.

Once the child feels secure in her relationship with her mother and has been able to disengage from the role reversal, short-term father-child therapy can be beneficial. As with the mother-child therapy, the objective is to establish a supportive relationship and to clarify role confusion. Many of the same conflicts cited in the mother-child relationship exist here and must be worked through to resolution. A therapeutic objective is to help the father and daughter to acknowledge the betrayal that occurred in their relationship and then to mourn the loss of trust. For although a rich, rewarding, and nonexploiting relationship may be established, trust will never be completely restored. Therapeutic techniques to facilitate this disengagement from role reversal will be dictated by the age of the child and the circumstances of her abuse.

Until this time, the child's visits with the abusive parent have been supervised by a professional helper. The fourth family session establishes a visitation plan for unsupervised visits that may or may not be part of a reunification plan. The plan needs to be sensitive to the child's feelings of safety, and rules are needed. Visits should be structured to provide for the child's comfort in terms of frequency, duration, and location of visits. The function of the rules is to protect the family by eliminating all circumstances favorable to molestation, identified by the family's abuse pattern. The process of involving the family in planning enables them to function as a unit and to develop a sense of mastery over their future.

If the family's goal is to reunify, then it is necessary to outline the reunification plan at this time. The child's social worker, who will be reporting to the court on the family's progress in treatment, should be included in this session. The plan needs to define:

1. The period of time anticipated for reunification.
2. The frequency, duration, and types of visits that will occur until the father moves back in with the family.
3. The changes in behavior required for the plan to be approved by the court.

The plan should be put in writing and signed by the parents, the child's social worker, the therapists, and the children in the family.

After several family visits, a discussion-of-progress session can be held. Unlike other critical family sessions, discussion-of-progress sessions may occur a number of times, such as after several successful family visits, when a family member believes a visit was unsatisfactory, or when someone in the family has broken a ground rule. The frequency of these sessions is determined by the family's needs.

This is a particularly vulnerable time for the family. They are beginning to come together and practice new patterns of interacting. New behaviors feel awkward, change seems frightening, and most family members wonder if they can trust themselves and others to behave in these unfamiliar ways. Sometimes family members' fear and uncertainty can become so overwhelming that they test a situation to relieve anxiety. For example, a father may "forget" and walk into his daughter's room early in the morning, or a mother may suddenly have to go out for a while, leaving father and daughter alone, or the daughter may run to answer the telephone wrapped in just her bath towel. These people are testing the safety of the new family dynamic, not backsliding into old behavior. They need the assurance that help is available, that someone can and will identify inappropriate behavior, and that the therapist will be told a ground rule has been broken. They are concerned that the therapist might become angry and give up on the family or that they are the only ones in the family trying to change. The therapist should recognize this testing behavior as an expected step in the process of change.

But although the therapist recognizes the testing behavior, that behavior cannot be condoned or ignored. The family needs therapists who can provide reliable, ongoing support—therapists who can strongly confront the violation of ground rules as well as help celebrate the family's growth. The therapists must model positive parenting behavior by providing guidance, protection, and nurturance, which includes clear limit setting and warm support.

For the child, group therapy is preferable to intensive individual work at this phase for several reasons. One-to-one therapy is stressful to a child because she feels pressure to work; it reinforces the confidant and family-secret role she has been maintaining in the family system; and it often gives the child the message that there is something the matter with her so that she requires mental-health treatment.

Children have difficulty expressing their feelings in one-to-one therapy. In groups, they readily express anger or sadness for another group member when they hear an experience recounted. This discharge of feeling relieves stress for the child and can later be bridged to the child's own situation. By contrast, one-to-one therapy is extremely threatening to the child as well as difficult, because the intimacy of the therapeutic relationship resembles that of the parent-child relationship in which she was betrayed.

The group also provides a setting that facilitates the exploration of the child's ambivalent feelings. It is essential that children have a safe environment in which they can acknowledge their positive and negative feelings toward their parents. They perceive, quite accurately, that most people would consider them "sick" if they expressed love for their fathers and that they would be victimizing their mothers if they expressed anger toward them.

The therapist should encourage children to discuss the molestation incidents and their feelings about those incidents, since this process minimizes feelings of shame. Gestalt techniques have helped children to gain a sense of mastery over their lives and to lessen their feelings of helplessness. Although the children may have been questioned about sexually abusive behavior during the disclosure-panic phase, the objective then was to obtain information, not to explore how the children experienced the incidents.

## Assessment-Awareness Phase

| Family Member | Behavior | Underlying Feeling |
|---|---|---|
| Father and mother | *Blame victim* | This wouldn't have happened if the child weren't seductive. |
| | *Rationalization* | The child enjoyed it and wasn't hurt by it. |
| | | The child was learning about sex; who's better qualified to teach it? |
| | | Father: If my wife had been more sexually responsive . . . |
| | | It couldn't be helped because of compulsion, alcohol, possession, and so on. |
| | *Manipulation and flight to insight* | If I act sorry, the therapist/group will get off my case. |
| | | I've found God now; there's no need for therapy. |
| | *Awareness of pain to self, family, victim* | I don't want it to happen again, but I'm afraid it will. |
| | *Depression* | Father: No one will trust me again . . . ever. |
| | | Mother: I'll never be able to trust him again. |
| | *Hope* | I'm beginning to understand how this all got started; maybe we can change and be a family again. |
| Child victim | *Yearning for closeness with mother* | My father won't ever forgive me for telling. If I don't have Mom, I don't have anyone. |
| | *Depression* | I must be sick 'cause I really love my father; no one knows how I feel. |
| | *Suicidal thoughts and attempts, self-mutilation* | If it weren't for me, there would be no problem. |
| | | Nothing will ever change for me; no one will want to be my friend or marry me. |
| | *Sexual acting-out* | If I talk and act cool, no one will know how scared I am and how awful I feel. |
| | *Shame* | Everyone knows; they can tell by looking at me. |
| | *Anger toward father* | He used me. |

Until now, the children generally are too involved in protecting the family to discuss their feelings openly.

When working with these children, the therapist will be dealing with here-and-now feelings of depression and self-destructive behavior. Children need to be given as much information as possible regarding the family and social service department plans for them. This kind of intervention is one of the many used to help the child develop feelings of self-confidence and trust in others.

## RESTRUCTURE PHASE

The restructure phase of treatment occurs when the family has reunited and family members are creating, learning, and practicing ways to interact within their "new" family. In the ideal new family system, communication is open and honest, family members are appreciated for their unique qualities as well as their shared family qualities, and change is viewed as a normal, ongoing process in life. Conjoint family therapy is the treatment modality needed during this phase. The duration of treatment is eighteen months to two years.

The formal family session designed to discuss the adjustment following reunification is usually held in the family home two weeks after reunification. The purpose of the session is for the family to identify those situations during their first weeks together again when they felt nervous or anxious about the possibility of molestation taking place. This session reinforces the concept that all families have difficulties and that talking openly about their interpersonal conflicts is necessary for families wanting to prevent abuse.

A male-female co-therapy team is extremely useful in conjoint family therapy. This provides a diagnostic tool for observing how family members relate to the same and the opposite sex. It also provides an opportunity for parental transference and a model for growth toward a clear, assertive male-female relationship. The couple has difficulty sustaining denial and resistance when confronted by both therapists. When needed, one therapist is able to confront while the other is supportive. The co-therapists can validate each other's perceptions of the family's interactions after the sessions and can support one another. The neediness of sexually abusive families can be overwhelming for a therapist working alone. A point well made by Herman and Hirschman (1977) is that a male therapist often finds it difficult to empathize with the female victim, whereas a female therapist tends to identify with the victim. Both reactions limit effectiveness and indicate the need for a co-therapy team. The therapists should schedule regular peer consultation to help them gain new perspectives, receive validation, and vent frustrations.

It is essential that a therapist working with sexually abusive parents be able to use the language, tolerate misconceptions, and deal with denial. They must confront their own attitudes, value judgments, and biases. By focusing their compassion on the now grown-up abused children—the parents—they are able to cope with their feelings about the more recent abuse of the child.

During the restructure phase of treatment, it is important to delve into the past and to examine the dynamics of the families in which the parents were raised. Many parents have not been able to resolve their relationships with their own families of origin, even if their families are far away. They expend a great deal of energy trying to please their parents and often are attempting to satisfy their unmet needs from early childhood. Examining their families of origin helps parents to gain insight into their searching behavior, to vent old feelings related to their parents, and to understand their parents from an adult perspective.

After the parents have been able to separate emotionally from their families of origin, they are better able to strengthen the parent-child boundaries in the present family. They must learn to look to their spouses or partners for comfort and nurturance rather than to their children. Reinforcement of clear family roles in terms of decision making and authority is essential. The children need to learn that their parents are in charge and can take care of themselves; they do not require the children's protection.

Practicing assertiveness and communication skills will enable parents to talk about their feelings and to state their needs clearly. They will learn to hear, without extreme discomfort, expressions of resentment or appreciation. And they will no longer be fearful that expressing anger openly might lead to violence or abandonment.

Learning parenting skills is an important part of the restructure phase of treatment. The parents must learn the developmental needs of children and the normal stages of development. It is essential that parents learn, for example, that children need clear, consistent limits. Therapists teach the family and help them to practice nonsexual physical nurturing. Learning to go beyond coping and to really enjoy each other in work and in play is an important part of therapy. Many parents fear they will lose control of the family or their respect if they allow themselves to be playful, and so they cut themselves off from the pleasure they might find. By teaching, modeling, encouraging, and supporting, the therapist can help family members learn to enjoy each other.

Continuing to participate in group therapy helps individual family members to increase their self-esteem, to practice social skills, and to increase their feelings of mastery of their own lives. Family members can often be effective as peer crisis counselors to others in the disclosure-panic phase.

At this point in treatment, the responsibility for the sexual molestation is clearly understood by everyone concerned and can be verbalized by all family members. The offending parent takes full responsibility and can talk about how he abused the power of his parental role. The nonoffending spouse can acknowledge that she was emotionally unavailable so that the child felt unable to confide in her and in fact felt that the mother must be protected. The child clearly understands that the molestation was not her fault. She has learned that people can know what has happened, can understand, and can still care about her.

At this stage of treatment, the family is aware of the myriad factors that are part of the family system, factors that will protect them from again becoming an abusive system. Now communication is open, family roles are clearly delineated, parent-child boundaries are strong, the couple has learned to meet their own needs and the needs of their children, the family is no longer socially isolated, and all family members have learned to ask for help from others when needed.

When the family has made the gains outlined above, it is time to begin the process of termination. Treatment should never be terminated for a family involved in therapy for less than one year. Ideally, the process should last two to three years. Termination of treatment should be open rather than final. Just as good parents support their adolescent youngers' moves outside the home toward

## Restructure Phase

| Family Member | Behavior | Underlying Feeling |
|---|---|---|
| Father and mother | *Less rigidity and defensiveness* | I believe we can make it. I feel more in control. Other families have succeeded. |
| | *Father takes responsibility for abusive behavior* | I betrayed my family's trust. I abused the power I have. My child is not responsible. |
| | *Mother takes responsibility for poor parenting* | I was not available for my child to confide in me. I allowed my child to protect me. |
| | *Increase in self-esteem* | I'm important and feel OK about being a good provider, employee, friend, and so on. I can change, make new friends, learn new skills, and so on. |
| | *Differentiation from families of origin* | I can't change my parents or continue to strive for what I missed from them. They had their own stresses and problems. I can let go. |
| | *Increased parent-child boundaries* | We are a couple and can look to each other for comfort and nurturance. The children are children with their own needs. |
| | *Pleasure in parenting* | It's OK to have fun and play with them. I am still the parent. My role as a parent is important. |
| | *Expression of non-sexual affection* | I feel comfortable touching the children. It's open and safe now. |
| | *Increase in assertiveness* | It's uncomfortable to hear what others resent and what they appreciate. It's hard to get used to talking about how I feel and asking for what I need, but keeping it all in was worse. |
| | *Ability to reach out for help* | I don't think this could happen again. If I even thought it might be happening, I would be able to talk about it and get help. That feels safe. |

| Family Member | Behavior | Underlying Feeling |
|---|---|---|
| Child victim and siblings | *Hope for future* | It's not my fault. |
| | *Increase in self-esteem* | People can know, understand, and still care about me. |
| | *Power* | I don't have to protect my parents. |
| | | It's OK to love my parent and hate what my parent's done. |
| | | Mom won't abandon me if I show anger toward her. |
| | *Mastery* | I know I can tell my parent to stop if the sexual molesting recurs. |
| | | I know how to tell Mom if the sexual molesting recurs. |
| | | I know it was wrong, and I may not be able to say I can fully trust right now. But I feel much better, and my family seems to be opening up and growing. |

more independent functioning, so good therapists support abusive families' efforts to fly solo.

The family needs to receive clear assurances from the therapists that they can return any time, that they are welcome to return, and that they do not have to fail or make big mistakes to do so. Abusive parents are very sensitive to rejection, abandonment, and desertion. They often misinterpret support of independence as one or more of these.

The process of termination in conjoint family therapy will require several sessions, one of which will be the formal termination-of-treatment session described in detail in the next chapter. This formal session is a time to solemnly acknowledge the family's past pain, present growth, and future commitment. It is also a time to celebrate and to underscore the fact that professional resources will remain available to the family.

*Chapter Seven*

## Critical Family Sessions

### INTRODUCTION

Family sessions held to deal with issues critical to the goal of preventing further sexual abuse differ in the following respects from traditional family therapy:

1. They last as long as it takes the family to complete the agenda.
2. They use a male-female co-therapy team or more than two therapists.
3. They take place where the victim feels safest.
4. They have a clear agenda that must be strictly adhered to.
5. The therapists must be more assertive, directive, and controlling of the process than they may otherwise choose to be.

Critical family sessions are held to deal with the following issues:

1. To confront the sexual abuse openly for the first time as a family.
2. To define the family's pattern of abuse.
3. To outline the family's long-term and short-term goals.
4. To establish a visitation plan.
5. To discuss progress toward accomplishment of goals.
6. To discuss adjustment after the family is reunited.
7. To discuss termination of court-ordered treatment.

The sessions are listed in the order in which they should occur. Clearly, the risk to the child of further sexual abuse is lessened by the completion of each successive session's agenda. Each critical family session is described below, with special attention given to the necessary process and to the role played by the therapists.

## SESSION 1: CONFRONTATION

A family session held to discuss the sexual abuse openly for the first time is vital because it serves as a starting point for the family's commitment to become an open family system. The session should take place when the victim feels strong enough to confront her father. The session should last as long as it takes to complete the agenda—usually between two and four hours. It should take place where the victim feels safest.

Ideally, there should be two therapists, preferably a male-female co-therapy team. The family should be directed to sit in such a way that everyone can have eye contact with everyone else. The female therapist should sit next to the victim to offer support and protection. Neither parent should sit next to the victim.

The family attempts to accomplish two difficult tasks simultaneously during this session: to communicate openly for the first time and to discuss the sexual abuse for the first time. Their anxiety level will be high, and it will require much energy, persistence, and direction to initiate and maintain the process. The family will need a directive approach from the therapists because they are learning, step by step, how to communicate openly.

The session should start with definitions of purpose. Each family member should state what she or he believes the purposes of the session to be. Only when each person has done this should the therapists clarify and summarize. Do not assume that the family is then clear regarding the purposes of the session. Each member of the family should be able to identify the purposes correctly before the session proceeds. Such precautions not only serve to prevent confusion as the session proceeds but also teach the family how to initiate clear communication with one another and with others.

The next step is for the therapist to introduce the first topic: the victim's expression of her feelings about having been sexually abused. The therapists should direct the parents not to respond verbally while the child is talking. The therapist sitting next to the victim should offer reassurance with statements such as:

- "I'm right here to help you."
- "You can say anything you want."
- "I will hold your hand or put my arm on your shoulder if that will help. Do you want me to?"

If the child hesitates, the therapist can direct her to start at the beginning; for example: "Tell us when your father first molested you, how you felt about it, and go on from there. Talk about your feelings."

This part of the process serves two purposes. First, it identifies for everyone when and where the child was molested and in what ways she was molested; second, it allows the child, and forces the abusing parent, to deal with the true impact of the sexual abuse. The family is beginning to identify its abuse pattern so that all family members can be aware of what will have to change in their family's functioning in order to prevent future abuse. The molesting parent is forced to acknowledge the true effects of his molesting behavior on the child. It is difficult to continue to rationalize that "she wanted it" or "she liked it" when the victim declares, loudly and clearly, exactly the opposite. What often happens during this part of the process is that the father will break down (often when the child does) and cry and sob. *He needs to experience this pain. The therapists should not rescue him by trying to make him feel better.* If he never experiences the pain he has caused his child, he will be unable to control his future impulses to molest her. Guilt in the molesting parent is a powerful therapeutic tool. Experiencing it is a necessary part of the process for change.

As witness to the victim's expressions of pain about the molestation, the child's mother and siblings are provided with a realistic portrait of the molestation. This serves to establish empathy, which can be mobilized for future protection of all the children.

The father can be directed to respond to the victim's expression of her feelings when she has revealed all the forms of sexual abuse that have occurred. He can be directed by the male therapist with statements such as:

- "What was it like for you to hear _____ express how she felt?"
- "How did you feel while _____ was talking?"
- "What's going on inside you right now?"

Difficulty in defining and describing "feeling states" is not uncommon in molesting parents. Fear of intimacy, fear of rejection, and fear of loss are responsible for their unwillingness to risk emotional vulnerability. The father will, therefore, need support and modeling from the male therapist, who needs to be sitting next to the father to provide this.

It is important for the victim to separate her feelings about her father from her feelings about what he did to her. She may be unable to do so with any clarity at this session, in which case it is appropriate for her to state that she is ambivalent or confused. For example:

- "Sometimes I think I hate you, Dad."
- "I love you, Dad. But I hate the things you did to me."
- "I may have enjoyed the sex itself sometimes, but I hate the fact that you used me."
- "I love you for a lot of reasons, like _____ and _____. But I hate you for taking my childhood."

The next issue to be addressed is how the victim's mother and siblings feel about what has been disclosed thus far. The mother's reactions to what her daughter has said should be elicited first. If the mother becomes upset and is crying and unable to talk, the female therapist should sit next to her and offer support so that she can verbally share her reactions to what has been said. Support can be offered with statements like: "It has not been easy to hear what your daughter and your husband have said. It is also not easy to talk about."

It is important that the mother explore in depth her feelings toward the abused child. This exploration must be guided by the therapist, who should be aware that the mother's first response is rarely an expression of her true feelings about the incident but rather what the mother thinks a "good" mother should say. The therapist can state that mothers often have complex, ambivalent feelings toward their daughters and can then help her to explore her feelings by providing a point of focus.

A directive from the female therapist to the mother to describe her feelings on hearing her daughter's disclosure provides such a focus. If the mother is vague or inconsistent in her statements, it may indicate that she feels ambivalent or confused about her daughter's statements. The therapist should ask her to clarify what she has said in such a case. If the mother's ambivalence centers around the veracity of the statements, as opposed to her feelings about them, then the mother may be unable or unwilling to protect the child in the future. It is not uncommon for mothers at this stage of treatment to feel ambivalent toward their daughters; mothers of incest victims frequently feel ambivalent toward all females, including themselves. If in fact the mother feels ambivalent toward the daughter, she should get permission to say so from the therapists. Permission can be offered with statements such as:

- "Feelings are not good or bad; they are just feelings."
- "Feelings are not always either black or white."

When the mother makes statements about her relationship to her daughter like "I feel I failed her," she should be directed to make such statements directly to her daughter. Such directives help to establish a new pattern of interaction between mother and daughter and may develop a new bond. The daughter should have the opportunity to respond to the statements her mother made. Part of the interchange here should focus on the "hints" that the daughter gave her mother about the incest. For example, if the mother states she now understands why her daughter asked to go along on shopping trips (since the father would molest her when the mother was out shopping) and that this realization makes her feel stupid and makes her wonder what other "hints" she missed, the therapists should ask the daughter to tell her mother what other hints she gave. The daughter should also be directed to tell her mother how she felt when her hints were not picked up.

When the victim's mother describes her feelings toward her husband after hearing him clearly validate the victim's statements, she needs full permission to be outraged with him. If the mother is resistant to expressing anger toward the husband, her ability and willingness to protect the children in the future should be seriously questioned. In fact, it can safely be assumed that she will *not* act to prevent future abuse. Her inability to express anger indicates that she is fully immersed in the victim role herself and is resigned to it.

Any declarations from the mother that she wants nothing more to do with the father, or that she wants the quickest divorce possible, or that she will prevent him from ever seeing the children again, should be countered immediately by the therapists with directives aimed at refocusing the process on her *feelings* about her husband rather than what *action* she is going to take against him. This is important because, under these circumstances, the victim is perceived by herself and the rest of the family as the one responsible for the threatened divorce, loss of the father, and destruction of the family. Such statements from the mother validate the victim's greatest fear prior to disclosure: that if she reports the incest, the family will be destroyed. The father should then be given the opportunity to respond to what his wife has said.

The siblings should each be directed by the therapist of the same sex to respond to what has been disclosed by the victim, if they are over the age of twelve. Children under the age of twelve may respond better to the support and guidance of the female therapist, who may be viewed as a mother figure. If the children are old enough to talk (age three and over), they are old enough to participate and should be required to do so. Children are at risk only if they are ignorant of the inappropriateness of molestation and what to do if it happens to them. Therefore, it is important to talk with the children who were not molested about the incest that occurred in their family, in language children can understand. This part of the session may be time-consuming, but it is the most effective way to begin to offer protection from sexual abuse to all the children.

All the children must be able to describe, in their own words, what they understand the child victim to have experienced. For example, a seven-year-old might say that "Daddy put his pee-pee in sister's thing between her legs." Each child must also be able to say how the victim felt about what was done to her. Many siblings feel jealous of what they perceive as a special relationship between the victim and her father and feel no sympathy toward her. Changing their perceptions of the real effects of the molestation serves to correct their damaged relationship to the victim. This process helps to establish the children as allies, joined to work toward the common goal of preventing the sexual abuse of anyone in the family.

When this part of the process is accomplished, the agenda for this session is completed. The therapists should then summarize the process and congratulate the family members on their hard work. The difficulty of the tasks they mastered needs to be acknowledged, as does the commitment they have made to become an open, trusting, and caring family. The symbolic meaning of a unity or celebration exercise at the end of the session is immeasurable. Standing in a circle with hands joined and expressing thanks to each other for participating is an effective closure. A more joyful and exhilarating exercise is to applaud everyone's efforts together while yelling, as if cheering at a football game, "Yea us! Yea us!"

## SESSION 2: DEFINING THE ABUSE PATTERN

The second family session should take place two to four weeks after the confrontation session. It is assumed that the parents and the victim are involved in ongoing therapy, where they can discuss in more depth their own reactions to the confrontation session. Parents often feel overwhelmed, frightened, and depressed after the confrontation session, whereas the children, especially the victims, feel exhilarated by the experience. They all need strokes for having accomplished the goals of the session and encouragement to continue to work toward preventing further sexual abuse. A pause of two weeks allows for at least one supportive session with their individual, couple, or group therapists. It also provides a breather from the intensity of interaction during the session. The short break allows everyone to recuperate emotionally. The break should not last more than three or four weeks, however, because the second critical family session requires review of some facts presented by the victim at the confrontation session. If many weeks have elapsed, time and energy will be spent recalling old material instead of eliciting "new" memories.

The session needs to take place in a neutral setting where the victim feels safe. Again, a male-female co-therapy team offers the advantages of identification and healthy role and interaction modeling for the family. The victim should sit next to the therapist she gets the most support from or feels the most rapport with. She should sit across from her father. The two therapists need to sit where they can maintain eye contact with one another.

The first order of business is to define the goals of the session, as was done in the confrontation session. The therapists need to explain the function of defining the family's particular abuse pattern. Some useful example phrases are:

* "If everyone knows how and when the molestation happened before, then everyone can do something to keep it from happening again."

- "If everyone knows what led up to the molestation before, then everyone can learn to recognize the signs and prevent it in the future."

The male therapist should direct the father to provide the first example of a molestation incident. The father should be instructed to describe the circumstances that provided the opportunity for molestation. The following information should be provided:

1. When did the incident occur? This information should be given in reference to some meaningful fact, such as the victim's age at the time, whether it occurred around a special occasion, holiday, or celebrated event.
2. Where did the incident occur? In whose house?
3. Who else was present? Who was absent?
4. What time of the day or night was it?
5. What room of the house did it occur in?
6. How long a period of time did the incident take?
7. Over the total period of time (months or years) that the incest occurred, how often was it possible to repeat the molestation because of favorable circumstances?

All of this information gives everyone a good idea of what they did (or did not do) to contribute to the favorable circumstances.

The victim then needs to be directed to think back to the incident described by her father, or a similar one, and say what changes in the family would help protect her under similar circumstances. For example, if her father always molested her during the night in her own bedroom, she might suggest having a lock put on her door. Or if he molested her when her brother was outside playing, she could have her brother agree to stay inside with her whenever she asks him to. If she was molested while her mother was out shopping, she can ask her mother to agree to take her along whenever she asks. Better yet, her mother can pledge not to go shopping without her if it would mean leaving her at home alone with her father.

Each of the favorable circumstances must be connected to the overt action by or the absence of a member of the family. The family must reach a solution for abolishing each of the circumstances. Only when this has been accomplished should the session continue.

The victim should be directed to describe the circumstances of an abusive incident different from the one described by her father but alike in that it was repeated many times over the years. She too should be instructed to provide the same kinds of information outlined previously. The same examination and resolution process should be followed with her example.

After the victim and the father have reviewed all the variations of circumstances under which molestation occurred, the therapists should ask the rest of the family if any of them recall witnessing molestation incidents. If any of them recall an incident, they should be instructed to describe it, providing the same facts outlined above. The same process followed with the other incident examples should be adhered to with the witnessed incidents. The victim should be asked to recall the incident and whether or not it was ever discussed with the witness.

The last part of the session should be spent summarizing the list of special circumstances that make up the family's molestation pattern. Each member of the family should be instructed to offer one item for the list. Some written record of the list should be kept for use at a later session.

A closure exercise recognizing everyone's participation and contribution is a fitting way to end the session.

## SESSION 3: OUTLINING GOALS

Session 3 needs to take place after the legal aspects of the case have been resolved. Since two court systems are usually involved, juvenile court and superior court, it may take three to six months to reach resolution. The family members should be in therapy from the time the report of incest is made. They benefit not only from the support and counseling but also from contact with other sexually abusive family members not experiencing the crisis of disclosure. Only when the crisis is over can the family think clearly about its alternatives. The time it takes to complete the legal process allows the family to become aware of its choices and the consequences attached to each.

This session needs to take place even if decisions regarding the future of the family have been made informally. The ritual and process of making choices together is a valuable learning experience. The family may want the social worker supervising the children for the court to be included in the session to answer questions about the court's expectations of them.

Since the agenda is in part to deal with official business related to the courts, it should take place either in the therapists' office or in the supervising social worker's office. Family members should be directed to sit wherever they wish to. The family has probably informally discussed their plans for the future, and if there are differences of opinion, they are likely to be represented in the seating arrangement. The professionals should not sit next to one another but should be able to maintain eye contact.

The family needs to define its short-term and long-term goals. Short-term goals are those that can be accomplished in six months to one year. Long-term goals require a year or more to accomplish. Short-term goals include:

1. Setting up visitation with family members living outside the home.
2. Staying in therapy.
3. Establishing rules to help prevent sexual abuse.
4. Participating in family recreational activities.

Long-term goals include:

1. Reunifying the family.
2. Getting a divorce.
3. Staying in therapy.
4. Preventing sexual abuse within the family.

The professionals need to explain the time frame for short- and long-term goals to the family. Each family member should be directed to offer one short- and one long-term goal for the list. How each goal is to be reached can be discussed after the lists of goals are completed. There is likely to be more discussion of the goals that the family did not discuss previously among themselves. The family should be allowed to struggle for a reasonable period of time without guidance so that their problem-solving skills can be accurately assessed. When the family meets at a later time to review their progress toward accomplishing their goals, the professionals can measure their improvement in the problem-solving area by calling their attention to their first efforts at joint decision making.

One of the professionals, acting as an observer, can write down the decisions the family makes. When the family determines that it has completed the task, the goals should be read aloud to them slowly and a vote taken on the inclusion of each goal.

When this process has been completed, the professionals need to give feedback to the family on their work. If the professional representing the court plans to report back to the court on the results of the session, the family needs to hear a clear statement of what will be reported and what recommendations will be made.

## SESSION 4: ESTABLISHING A VISITATION PLAN

A family session to set up a schedule of visits and rules outlining what is and is not permissible during visits should take place before *any* unsupervised visits are allowed. Visits are supervised when a professional helper (social worker, probation officer, or therapist) is present to observe the interaction.

Whether a visitation schedule is part of a reunification plan or not, it needs to be sensitive to the child's feeling of safety. For this reason, visits should be structured to provide the utmost protection to the child. The child's comfort should be used to gauge the spacing, duration, and location of the visits.

The therapists begin the session by clarifying with all family members the agenda for the session. They explain that the ground rules for the visits are dictated by the expectations of the court and the victim's comfort with the visits. The family needs to be given the opportunity to discuss their feelings about this arrangement.

If the family has had several supervised visits and these have been satisfactory, then several half-day unsupervised visits might be suggested. The family needs to be directed to assume responsibility for scheduling these visits and deciding what they want to do together. When they have done so, it should be explained to the family that all-day unsupervised visits will be scheduled only if the half-day visits go well. The supervising professional will meet with the family after several half-day visits to discuss their success.

All-day visits can be scheduled tentatively so that the family can complete a long-range visit schedule. The therapists need to explain that three or four satisfactory all-day visits must take place before the father can spend weekends with the family (without sleeping overnight in the home). The family is directed to make a tentative schedule of such weekend visits. The next phase the therapists present is overnight visits by the father. The therapists state that there should be a minimum of four weekend visits that incorporate overnight stays before a short trial period of reunification is recommended.

The process of actively involving the family in their own future serves to give them a greater sense of control of their destiny, gives them the opportunity to function as a unit, and lends credibility to their long-range goals. As their plans for the future take shape on the calendar, they begin to perceive their hopes in more concrete terms; their future together or apart begins to be real.

After the scheduling of a week-long trial reunification, the family is ready to begin discussing the second agenda item: establishing ground rules for all visits. The function of the rules is to provide maximum protection to the victim by eliminating all circumstances favorable to molestation. The family's abuse pattern serves as a guide for defining the ground rules. The therapists must explain the need for ground rules to the family and direct them to use their abuse pattern to set up rules for visits. Some sound ground rules follow:

1. Visits must include the whole family.
2. Bedrooms are off limits at all times to the parent who molested.
3. The mother must accompany the children throughout the visits, including transporting them to the site of the visit.
4. The molesting parent may not take one child alone to use the bathroom.
5. The molesting parent may not bathe or dress children for a visit.

The victim needs to be asked to suggest some ground rules that would make her feel safe from any molestation attempts during visits. Even if the protection offered by her suggested rules is evident to no one but herself, her rules should be included in the list. The therapists should add any rules that they feel are important.

Additionally, the family should be told that a session will be held immediately should anyone break a ground rule.

When the family has completed the list, it should be read aloud and a vote taken on its acceptability to all. If all agree on the rules, the date, time, place, and activity of their first visit should be announced. The family should receive supportive feedback from the therapists on the accomplishment of the session's task and encouragement to proceed with positive attitudes toward their first goal.

## SESSION 5: DISCUSSION OF PROGRESS

The first discussion of progress should take place after the family has had several successful day visits or as soon as any family member feels that a visit was unsatisfactory. It is important to have sessions for discussing the family's progress because:

1. Ongoing therapeutic support will help them continue to do well.
2. Therapy should not be associated only with problems and mistakes.
3. Unhappy and abusive families are often uncomfortable with things going smoothly or turning out well and need encouragement not to "program" failure.
4. Regular review of the process of change will help the family to lessen anxiety about it.
5. Abusive families need regular contact with people significant to them, since they often perceive a lack of contact as abandonment.
6. Abusive family members have difficulty making their needs known. Frequent opportunities to speak up must be provided to prevent a problem from becoming a crisis.

If a session is held after someone in the family has broken one of the ground rules for visits, the rule breaker must be confronted strongly. Often a former victim will break a ground rule to test her safety. For example, the child may ask the parent who molested her to tuck her into bed. Such setups need to be discussed, especially if the family's goal is reunification, since the frequency and variety of these attempts is likely to increase. The child should be encouraged to say to the parent she set up something like: "I need to know if you've changed. I needed to know I was safe." The parent also needs to express his feelings about having been set up.

When someone breaks a ground rule, all family members should be required to tell that person what the infraction caused them to experience emotionally. The therapists should handle the situation much as a good parent disciplines a child—by expressing disappointment in the person, stating clearly the unacceptability of the infraction, setting a penalty to fit the violation, and expressing belief in the will of the person not to repeat the behavior.

Obviously, if a child was molested, visits should cease immediately, the plan to reunite the family should be canceled, and the incident should be reported to the authorities. More often than not, ground rules are broken to test the professionals' commitment to the family. The process of change is in large part a reparenting process, with the professionals acting as surrogate parents. It is therefore reassuring to have the professionals respond immediately, *as they stated they would,* to any violation of the ground rules. If the professionals do not follow through, the family will lose trust in them, and the end result will likely be the abandonment of their long-range goals.

Ideally, sessions to discuss progress should be scheduled after each phase of the visitation plan is completed. There should be sessions after three or four half-day visits, after four all-day visits, after four weekend visits, and after a one-week trial reunification period. It is frightening and anxiety-provoking for the family to change their interaction patterns, their communication systems, and their functioning as a family unit simultaneously. Such effort demands and deserves *strong, reliable, and ongoing support.* Dependency during this middle phase of treatment is appropriate and should not be discouraged. More independent maintenance of the new patterns of behavior and attitudes can safely be encouraged after the family's confidence has been reinforced over a period of months by repeated experiences of goal achievement. When a family completes each phase of the visitation plan without incident and is rewarded with support and encouragement, the family's chances for successfully accomplishing its goals multiply.

When a goal seems unreachable in terms of time and effort, the family is much more likely to resist making any effort to achieve it.

However, when a task is difficult but encouragement, guidance, and support are provided consistently throughout the efforts made to accomplish the task, the likelihood that it will be successfully accomplished increases.

The therapists need to stroke the family for discussing their progress honestly. They should interpret this progress as evidence of the family's emotional growth. The tentative date of the next progress discussion session should be announced.

## SESSION 6: DISCUSSION OF ADJUSTMENT FOLLOWING REUNIFICATION

The family that reunites needs repeated acknowledgments from professionals that *all* families experience problems from time to time and that denial of such problems is therefore suspect. The reason such realities need to be repeated to sexually abusive families is that abusive parents are likely to set an unrealistic standard of perfection for themselves. Abusive parents often have abusive parents themselves who were overly critical of them throughout childhood. The critical parenting experienced is internalized, and the parenting pattern is repeated in the next generation. It is therefore essential to keep in mind that the abusive parents are being reparented while they learn how to parent more appropriately themselves.

There are two important goals for this family session: the family should begin to value its strengths and to accept its limitations. Becoming accustomed to talking openly about interpersonal conflicts is necessary for families wanting to prevent abuse. Only in a family system with open communication can the children be assured of safety. The children must feel comfortable expressing their feelings to their parents and must be able to trust that they will be heard. If such communication is unknown to the children, they lack the most important resource for their protection—the protection available on request from either parent.

Session 6 can take place in the therapists' office or in the family home. The advantage of having it in the family home is that incidents can be more easily recalled and reenacted there. The session can begin with the therapists asking the family members to think back on their first week reunited and to identify one situation in which they felt nervous or anxious about the possibility of molestation taking place. The therapists should pause for a few minutes to give them time to isolate an incident in their minds. They should then ask if everyone has chosen an incident. If all have, they direct the ex-victim to relate her incident to the group. Her ability and willingness to relate such information is a good indication of her ability to report her own abuse anxiety. Her inability to do so indicates the necessity to provide her with more intensive individual assertiveness training. She must be able to participate in her own ongoing protection.

The incident should be described to the group in the same manner that she identified molestation incidents to the family in the pattern-of-abuse session. She should describe the situation, her feelings about it, and what she would change to relieve her anxiety and fear. The following is an example of such an incident description:

It was Saturday morning. Mom had gone to the store. Everyone was asleep. I was watching cartoons on TV. I was lying on the rug on my stomach. Dad came into the room. He had on a bathrobe. He sat down on the rug in a way that I could see he wasn't wearing anything underneath the bathrobe. I could see his penis and got scared but couldn't think of what to say or do.

The therapists need to encourage discussion of why the child (or whoever is relating the incident) was unable to talk about it to the family *at the time it occurred*. The incident can be reenacted, and various alternative methods of initiating discussion of feelings around it can be role played. This is a problem-solving technique useful to families learning to communicate openly. All members of the family should role play the incident. Only by experiencing the situation will family members give it personal meaning.

The session should not end until each family member can give one example of a situation in which she or he was aware that circumstances were favorable to molestation. The family should receive positive feedback on their efforts to communicate honestly with one another and should be encouraged to continue their work. A closing exercise is appropriate.

## SESSION 7: TERMINATION OF TREATMENT

The formal termination-of-treatment session with the family will not signify the end of treatment but rather will mark the end of the active restructure phase. As stated earlier in the text, it is essential that the family be given assurance that therapeutic resources are always available to them. These resources can range from consultation to individual sessions to intensive conjoint family therapy.

The family should have a major part in planning who they wish to have present at the meeting and when and where this meeting should occur. They should plan, with the guidance of the therapists, the style, content, and format of this final session. The focus of the meeting is to acknowledge and appreciate the family's hard work and growth and to reaffirm their commitment to nurture the family and to deal openly and honestly with difficulties as they arise.

This time of closure will be emotionally laden for all. Therefore the wishes of the family should dictate the style of the session. This meeting should allow time for each person present to express his or her feelings, for quiet contemplation, and perhaps for celebration. We have had families commemorate this event with candles, poems they have written, and food they have prepared. It is a time when therapists, too, silently reaffirm their commitment.

---

## Chapter Eight

# Treatment of a Sexually Abusive Family: A Case Study

This chapter describes the treatment of a dysfunctional family that came into contact with public social service agencies because of sexual abuse. This case study was selected because it demonstrates effective family treatment even though the child protective service workers did not have the benefit of an established child sexual abuse treatment program.

## THE FAMILY

### The Children

Lisa is a pretty, vivacious four-year-old girl with long, blond hair and large, sparkling blue eyes. She is a needy child who clings to adults with constant chatter and overtures for close body contact. With adult males, Lisa is coy and flirtatious—a parody of an adult female "vamp." She interacts with adult women as if she were a peer. Lisa does not have playmates. Her play is restricted and focused primarily on her Barbie dolls and on her four-month-old sister, Marla, who is the child of her mother and Leon. Lisa lives with her mother, "Daddy Leon," and her sister and frequently spends time with her maternal grandparents.

### The Mother

Susan, Lisa's birth mother, is an attractive twenty-three-year-old woman who successfully manipulates others with her helpless

childlike manner and her ever present smile. The denial and minimization she uses to defend herself against pain are evident when
she reports her past physical and sexual abuse and her years of
growing up in various foster homes. Smiling, she states: "It wasn't
so bad. Dad didn't really know what he was doing, and Mom, well,
she hit me a lot, but I usually deserved it."

Susan is the youngest of five children. She was placed in foster
care from ages nine through fourteen for what she describes as her
inability to get along with anyone: "Sometimes I just blew up for no
reason." She returned home at age fourteen: "I tried real hard to get
along with my mom this time. Dad, well, he was drunk most of the
time, and I just stayed away from him."

At seventeen, Susan became pregnant, married her child's father,
John, and moved into an apartment with him a block away from her
parents' home. Susan describes John as a good person. "Even
though we've been divorced, he still brings me things and comes by
to see if I'm OK. I guess we broke up because I started to drink—I
don't do that now. But sometimes he didn't know what to do, so he
hit me."

Another man, Leon, moved in with Susan and Lisa shortly after
the marital separation. Susan describes Leon as a good provider
and loving father. "I stopped drinking for him," she said. "He
doesn't ever hit me. When he gets real mad, he just goes out and
drives around, but he always comes back." Susan says that Leon
was really pleased when Marla was born. "He's working two jobs
now just so he can get a real house for his three girls."

## The Father

Leon, Susan's live-in partner, is a quiet, slightly built twenty-five-
year-old. His primary interests are his family and his car. Although
he works fifty hours a week, he finds no satisfaction in working
apart from the salary he receives. Leon is a loner. He avoids eye
contact with others, his conversation is hesitant, and he is obviously
uncomfortable in social situations.

Leon was raised by his mother and two older sisters. His father
died when he was five years old. Talking about his childhood, Leon
said, "My mother took good care of me; ah . . . I never got hit or
nothing. She'd get real lonely sometimes but always stayed home

with us kids." He stated that he maintains a close relationship with his mother and often goes to see her and performs maintenance chores at her home.

When discussing his present family situation, Leon focuses on his plans to buy things for the family. He comments that Susan is a good mother who sometimes gets overwhelmed and needs his help with the girls. "I guess the only problem we have is that she lets Lisa stay at her grandparents a lot. I mean, we're a family here, and I think she shoudn't spend so much time away."

## EVENTS PRECEEDING TREATMENT

Lisa, age four, was admitted to the pediatric ward of the hospital with a diagnosis of gonococcal arthritis, an advanced stage of gonorrhea. Medical reports were forwarded to the Department of Public Health. The health department subsequently administered tests to the child's mother, Susan. The test results were inconclusive, since Susan had been taking antibiotics for the flu. As a precaution, Susan was treated for gonorrhea. She told a public health nurse that she had no idea how her child contracted the disease but thought that "it must have been someone in the neighborhood." Lisa remained in the hospital for ten days of treatment and was brought back to the hospital on two occasions for scheduled follow-up visits. On verification that treatment had been completed, Protective Services closed the case.

Six months later Susan contacted the police, reporting that she awoke in the night to find Leon over Lisa's bed. Her daughter was lying face down, her legs spread apart and her panties removed. Susan ran to the neighbors crying, "He raped my baby!" Statements were taken by the police, and Leon was arrested. Lisa was taken to the emergency room of the hospital for examination. The medical report showed no signs of sexual assault. However, Lisa told the examining physician that Daddy Leon touched her genitals and that he had done this on other occasions.

Susan and Leon's mother went to the District Attorney's office the following day. Susan signed a complaint, and both women asked if therapeutic help could be arranged for Leon. They were told that Leon denied the allegation, that a child as young as Lisa was not considered a credible witness, and, since Susan did not actually see sexual abuse occur, there would be no criminal charges filed against Leon. Leon was released from custody, moved out of the family home, and went to live with his mother. It was later disclosed in treatment that he did this because a very angry police officer had privately told him that "he had better stay away from Lisa."

Child Protective Services, following up on the police report, felt that without the court's protection, Lisa was in danger of further sexual abuse because Leon could move back into the home at any time—a likely possibility, since he was the father of Marla, Lisa's four-month-old sister. Also, research shows that often the "non-abusive spouse will seek out, consciously or unconsciously, a mate that has the potential to abuse" (DeFrancis 1968). Furthermore, the literature on the sexual abuse of children clearly points to the nonabusive parent's role in the abusive situation (DeFrancis 1968; Kaufman, Peck, and Tagiuri 1954; Lustig et al., *Archives*, 1966). Incest is seen as a problem in a family system; each member has a role in initiating, tolerating, and perpetrating the abuse (Eist and Mandel 1968; Gutheil and Avery 1975; Lustig et al., *Archives*, 1966; Machotka, Pittman, and Flomenhaft 1967). Until the filing of a petition in this matter, the courts tended to concern themselves solely with the victim and the abusive parent and did not recognize the abuse as the result of a dysfunctional family system. The petition filed in Lisa's behalf cited literature establishing the family dynamics involved in child sexual abuse.

The juvenile court judge ordered that Lisa be made a court de-pendent with a dependency review to occur in one year. During this year, Lisa would remain in her mother's care under the supervision of the Child Welfare Department. The judge directed Susan to seek therapeutic help and to ensure that Lisa would have no further contact with Leon.

One might legimately question why public agencies did not take immediate steps to protect Lisa when it first became apparent that she had been abused. From our experience, we believe that this is an example of the professional community's denial of the preva-lence and seriousness of child sexual abuse. Each case is perceived in isolation, and therefore efforts are not made to change policies and procedures to protect these children more effectively.

## DISCLOSURE-PANIC PHASE

Therapy for Susan was provided by a social worker from the Family Therapy Unit of Child Protective Services. For the first month, they met twice weekly and then once a week at Susan's home. Susan was in crisis. She became despondent, felt overwhelmed by having to care for her children without Leon's help, and believed there were no solutions for her present difficulties.

She initially expressed anger toward Leon, stating, "How could he do this to me?" and "My mother will really have it in for me now." At the same time, Susan said that she was terrified of losing Leon. Crisis therapy techniques were used to help Susan take charge of her life and understand that she was not alone and would survive this ordeal.

Susan and her therapist arranged for Lisa to attend a small nursery school in the neighborhood, and provision was made for the therapist to provide weekly consultation to those working directly with Lisa. Fortunately, the nursery school had a male psychology student intern who, together with the teacher, accepted the responsibility of providing for Lisa's needs.

Lisa's social worker determined that Lisa needed to learn skills to establish peer relationships, build self-esteem, learn age-appropriate roles, and learn to relate to adult males in a nonseductive manner. Lisa was the "little mother" in the family home. She would answer the door, greet the guests, and ask if they wanted coffee or beer. She took charge of the baby, telling her mother when it was time for her to be fed and so on. The program helped to teach Lisa how to be a little girl. The intern gave Lisa an opportunity to work through some of her feelings about the loss of Daddy Leon and about her past sexual activities. This was done primarily through play therapy sessions.

Treatment for the victims of child abuse is often sabotaged by the child's parents, whose narcissistic needs bring on jealousy when the child gets more attention than they do (Mirandy 1976). For this reason, the nursery school program was initially presented as a way for Susan to obtain respite from the constant care of Lisa. Actually, the reverse was intended: Lisa had a few hours a day during which she was not expected to meet her mother's needs.

Leon was contacted by a male therapist from the Family Therapy

Unit and advised that therapeutic help was available for him. He said that he was not interested. His response was understandable, since accepting the offer would be admitting to a criminal offense.

## ASSESSMENT-AWARENESS PHASE

The therapist's role with Susan was to reparent, that is, to engage in a relationship in which there is caring, clear limit setting, and, for a period of time, dependency. The therapist worked through Susan's initial distrust and testing and prepared herself for the subsequent dependency that follcwed when trust began to build in their relationship. Much support was needed at this time because of Susan's fears of living without a male partner in the home.

Susan, who was sexually molested as a child by her father, was invited to join a therapy group for women who had similar histories of sexual abuse. Although transportation and child care were provided, Susan found reasons for frequent absences. She used the group to exact sympathy for what she believed was her completely innocent role in her daughter's abuse. Although she spoke of the sexual abuse she experienced as a child, it was reported with no outward sign of emotion. Susan energetically protected her father's image during these sessions. She dismissed her mother's role and denied any relationship with the current situation of Lisa's abuse. When confronted with Leon's abuse of Lisa, she pleaded for sympathy and understanding for Leon from the group. But the group was valuable for Susan because for the first time she developed warm and fairly close relationships with other women. She stated during one session: "I've always felt so different from other women. . . . I never thought I'd meet anyone who could really understand what it [the abuse] was like for me."

Throughout the following months, whenever Susan told her therapist or group leader how Leon was misunderstood and how she wanted to "forgive and forget," she was told that couple therapy was available for them. Shortly after Lisa mentioned to her teacher, in front of her mother, that they had visited Daddy Leon, Susan called her therapist and asked if she and Leon could both be seen in therapy. Susan was told firmly that she had ignored the court's directive and that her action would be reported to the court.

The therapist arranged to see Susan that same day to provide emotional support. After being advised of the situation, the juvenile court judge arranged to meet with Susan and her therapist in his chambers. He advised her of her responsibilities and told her she could meet with Leon, but Lisa must not be present. He stated that he did not believe that she should leave the baby with Leon either. He sternly told her that Lisa would be removed from her home if there were further infractions.

The male therapist contacted Leon by telephone to offer individual therapy until the two therapists thought it was appropriate for them to come together for couple therapy. He focused on the positive intent of Leon's wanting to reestablish his role as a family member, and he spoke about sexual misuse as a serious problem that affected families. Leon was supported for his courage and for caring for his family. He was also told what he might generally expect to happen in the course of treatment. The therapist further stated that although many men think about canceling their appointments, those who follow through do not regret their decision.

Leon saw the therapist weekly in individual therapy sessions for the next two months. During this time, the therapist contacted the district attorney's office and explained the circumstances. He was advised that they did not want to bother with this case even if, in a therapeutic session, Leon admitted to the abuse. They would, however, be willing to meet with Leon and tell him they would not take legal action as long as he was involved in treatment. The therapist arranged to accompany Leon to the meeting in the district attorney's office, thereby establishing a more supportive relationship with him. This also freed Leon to discuss the molestation of Lisa when he was able to do so. (It is possible that, had Leon consulted an attorney at this point, the treatment process would likely have been stopped.)

In individual therapy for Leon, the therapist both confronted Leon's abusive behavior and provided him with emotional support. Leon spoke of his need for Susan and his fear that she would never let him return to the family home. At the same time, he expressed anger toward her, blaming her for the sexual abuse. "If she'd not been so fucking shut off, you know. . . . she's a tease, that's what. Well, I don't think it would have happened if, you know, she'd been like a real woman should be." The therapist continued to confront Leon's denials and rationalizations and prepared him for the family confrontation that was soon to come.


## Confrontation

The goal of this formal family session was to discuss the abuse openly for the first time with all members of the family and their therapists present. The purpose was to break through the denial process. Even though Leon could now say that he sexually abused Lisa, he minimized both the abuse and his responsibility. Susan too minimized the sexual abuse, in part, because she was still trying to make her own molestation by her father acceptable. The therapists had established enough of a relationship with Susan and Leon to push against their defenses.

Anxiety was high at the confrontation session. The parents, their therapists, the children, and Lisa's play therapist were present. Four-year-old child victims often do not experience the guilt and shame that older victims feel. Every effort was made to ensure that Lisa was prepared for this session and that it would be a positive experience for her. Because of her developmental stage and her limited verbal abilities, the therapist had to be patient with her rambling, disjointed responses and their irrelevant details. Anatomically correct stuffed dolls were used for demonstration. Lisa awkwardly described how Leon had her masturbate him, how he rubbed his penis between her legs, and how she had to swallow semen when she performed fellatio. Susan began choking and was close to vomiting, but she was not rescued. Leon became pale and his hands trembled. Lisa poignantly stated that she would rather have had Leon play Barbies with her or read her a story.

The dialogue continued as the therapists talked to Lisa about touching and what is OK between adults and kids, explaining that her body belongs to her and so on. Lisa and her therapist went to play in another area of the room, while the adults' therapists continued by talking about the gonorrhea that had been in the family and its impact on Lisa.

Guilt is a powerful therapeutic tool in work with abusive families. In some instances it must be created in order to protect both the child and the parent. For the first time, Leon and Susan were able to gain some understanding of what had happened to their child.


## Beginning Couple Therapy

After several weeks in individual therapy, Leon and Susan began couple therapy with the therapists they had been seeing individually. The primary focus in these sessions was on the couple relationship: how they were coping with living apart, how they dealt with the loneliness, and how they reacted to those in their respective families who were aware of the incest behavior. Some time was spent exploring what attracted them to each other when they first established their relationship, followed by a discussion of what they appreciated about themselves and each other. Both Susan and Leon exhibited passive-dependent behavior—she demonstrated a placating style of communication; his was that of a quiet, passive blamer. Leon had difficulty expressing feelings and tended to withdraw emotionally when he felt anxious. Susan would rush in and talk for him, explaining how he felt. When she became anxious, her smile became brighter, and she tried to shift the focus.

The couple's way of relating to the co-therapy team elicited important diagnostic information. Susan behaved toward the male therapist like a charming, bright child. She responded with a constant smile and nodded her head to anything the female therapist said in a way that thinly disguised her hostility. Leon appeared aloof from both therapists; however, he sat close to the male therapist, began to repeat the therapist's statements as his own, and by the third week, began to grow a beard (the male therapist was bearded). Leon constantly watched the female therapist with a pleading intensity; his voice lowered and sounded infantile when he responded to her. Both Leon and Susan exhibited passive-dependent and immature behavior, as well as communication patterns that were vague and distorted.

There was much evidence of an enmeshed couple system, as described by Minuchin (1974), and of a pseudomutuality in the relationship, as described by Wynne (1958). The tasks throughout therapy were for the couple to disengage emotionally, to overcome their resistance to change, to begin to assert openly to get their needs met, to establish parent-child boundaries, and to learn parenting skills. They were directed to keep journals. Their first homework assignment was to keep notes of "I" messages and of times when Susan spoke for Leon and he allowed this to happen. The notebook device helped make what was worked on in therapy part of their conscious awareness between sessions.

When the parents felt more at ease in the couple sessions, they spoke of conflicts in their relationship. Susan was able to verbalize her disappointment: "Whenever Leon touches me, it just means one thing—he wants sex." Leon said that he didn't know why she complained, since that was not very often. He became angry and blurted out that Susan would lead him on and then interrupt coitus before he ejaculated, crying that she could not continue because "she had been molested . . . by her father . . . when she was five years old." They spent several sessions sorting out the feelings behind Leon's incestuous behavior: revenge, loneliness, and so on. The therapists believed that Leon gained some insight into Susan's behavior and that Susan's energy was directed toward gaining some sympathy for her unhappy childhood. The therapists decided that it was time to focus on Susan and her family of origin.

## Susan and Leon's Family Histories

Initially, in these family-of-origin sessions, Susan began to report her incestuous experiences rapidly and without affect. The female therapist, using implosive therapeutic techniques, was able to assist her in experiencing the sadness that was beneath her defenses. She was able to cry for the child who so desperately needed affection that she frequently performed fellatio on her father in order to get "loving" attention. Gestalt and body therapy techniques were employed to recreate a specific scene in which she gained mastery over the situation by successfully warding off her father's seductive advances toward her and assertively demanding what she needed from him. Later, Susan was able to understand from an adult perspective the emotional blackmail that her father had used in the past. Her feelings of confusion, guilt, and responsibility for the sexual acts with her father lessened as she gained insight into her behavior.

In both these instances of cathartic release, the therapists assisted and supported Susan in connecting past survival patterns with her current behavior and the problems it caused. She spoke of her inability to express anger openly, of sleep disturbances, and of problems with overeating. Susan also had many somatic complaints involving her sex organs and vague stomach disorders.

The male therapist worked with Leon to gather information and explore his feelings about growing up in his family. Gestalt techniques were used to enable Leon to experience his feelings of sadness and sense of betrayal at his father's death when he was child and, later, to connect with his feelings of rage at the intrusive behavior of his mother and three older sisters. Eventually he was able to speak of the emptiness he experienced at being locked inside the walls he had built around himself.

The therapists noted that during Leon's early adolescence, his mother often drank excessively. The situation and the family dynamics indicated possible sexual abuse of Leon; however, the therapists believed that Leon was not yet emotionally ready to reach a deeper level of feeling. Time was spent bridging Leon's methods of coping in his family of origin with his relations to others in the present, especially to Susan. Attention was given to the high price he was paying for using former survival patterns.

The female therapist's task during these sessions was to be with Susan, to make occasional quiet comments both to support her and to assist her in developing insight. She also had to keep her from rescuing Leon, explaining that he needed to experience his anger and sadness. Leon began to learn how to ask Susan for emotional support. Susan was learning not to express Leon's feelings for him.

The family histories were explored in more depth so that both Susan and Leon could experience their parents from an adult perspective as people with unmet needs, fears, difficulties in relating, and so on. Leon and Susan were able to discuss the qualities and behaviors they liked in their parents and those they didn't like.

It was at this time, without prompting from the therapists, that Leon told of his confusion in growing up in an all-female household. His mother catered to what she called "the little man" in the family and insisted that his older sisters do the same. His sisters resented this and tormented him when their mother was not present. He described incidents when his mother was drinking and he'd become very uncomfortable when she'd show "affection." He told of times when she would sit on his bed late at night and talk for hours about his father: "I felt like I was supposed to do something, but I didn't know what." Leon was highly resistant to exploring this area any further. The male therapist supportively put his arm around Leon and told him that it was all right to say no to his mother. Leon acknowledged by shaking his head; he was silent after that and was close to tears. Susan quietly supported him and said that she had always envied Leon because it seemed to her that he always got what he wanted when he was growing up: "You were treated like a little prince."

The focus of treatment shifted to the here-and-now couple relationship, with occasional references made to family-of-origin material. The sessions were primarily supportive and integrative. The homework assignments were for each of them to make a same-sex friend separately and to find a recreational activity they could share. They continued throughout the sessions to write successful assertive incidents in their notebooks. Susan wrote pages about the small steps she had taken; Leon wrote tersely of some solid assertions he had made. Both were strongly supported for their efforts and encouraged to ask assertively for what they needed from each other.

### Leon's Crisis

Leon and Susan missed a scheduled session without explanation. During the week the therapists telephoned and discovered that Leon had moved out of his mother's home, was drinking, and had missed several days' work. They instructed Susan to have Leon contact the male therapist. It was decided that if Leon called he would have an individual session. This was held at Leon's apartment. Leon was extremely anxious and in crisis. The therapist gave him support for the move he had made, while acknowledging the pain of separation. Attention was given to the concrete steps Leon needed to take to keep his job as well as what he could do to help himself if he entertained suicidal thoughts.

The following sessions were used primarily to support Leon's success in separating from his mother as well as Susan's ability to care for herself emotionally during this process. The therapists and the couple touched some deep feelings, made up off-color limericks for the occasion, and sang victory songs.

Another cause for celebration was that Leon and Susan had gone bowling together. This was an important step in learning to have fun, taking care of themselves and their couple relationship, and being less isolated. They said that they were ashamed of their awkwardness. They knew they would never join a team but thought that just the two of them could go again if the therapists wanted them to. The therapists insisted.

## Restructuring and Termination

The final sessions of therapy focused on reinforcing the couple relationship, teaching and reinforcing parenting skills, and strengthening parent-child boundaries. Equal time was given in the sessions to the couple relationship, which usually began by discussing their bowling scores; the latter part of the session focused on parenting. This was sometimes painful, since it often reminded them of their own empty childhood years.

The therapists had refrained from using the words *Lisa* or *family* as part of the boundary-setting process. By this time in therapy, Leon and Susan were saying "my" or "our daughter" and "our couple relationship" automatically. With a great deal of prompting and support from the therapists (as well as a suggestion that it would look good on the court report) Leon and Susan joined a parenting class/discussion group that met weekly. Time in the sessions was spent supporting and reinforcing what they had learned as well as encouraging them to develop relationships within the group.

In a special session with the children, Leon and Susan separately and somewhat awkwardly told Lisa that until that time they had not been very good parents but that they had learned many things about themselves and were going to help themselves and her. The child did not really understand the implication; however, she grasped the seriousness of the situation and nodded solemnly. In another session with Lisa, there were incidents in which Leon and Susan played with her. When a situation arose that called for them to set limits to her behavior, they did so appropriately and were supported for their actions. The therapists suggested that the couple encourage their daughter to call Leon "Dad," and they did. Lisa responded happily—a new name for a new relationship.

Arrangements were made through the court for Lisa to be allowed to spend Saturdays with Leon, with the stipulation that her mother be present. These activities and interactions engendered more material to be used in the therapy sessions.

The juvenile court returned legal custody of Lisa to her mother. The couple terminated therapy, and Leon resumed living with Susan and the two children. A step that might further strengthen the parent-child boundary would be a legal marriage between Leon and Susan. A major step for Susan would be to separate emotionally from her parents, especially her mother. Susan is aware of this but is unable to do so at present.

Leon did not appear to empathize with Lisa's being sexually misused. His motivation in therapy continued to be his fear of Susan's terminating their relationship if the molestation continued. But both Leon and Susan know that there is room in their lives for growth, and they know how to obtain therapeutic assistance if they decide they need further help.

## CASE DISCUSSION

Gutheil and Avery (1975) divided the literature on the subject of incest into three conceptual phases:

1. Epidemiological-descriptive phase, when the child is seen as the victim of the parental sexual deviate.
2. Psychological-investigative phase, when incest is viewed as a collusive act in which a child is active-seductive and the parents are driven to repeat their childhood experiences and conflicts with a new generation.
3. Family-process phase, when the incest serves as a defense against loss and separation.

In Lisa's family, each of the above criteria applies.

Leon both feared and desired warmth and attention from a female. His family history suggests highly sexualized early relationships with his mother and three older sisters. His father's early death left him without a male figure in his life and with a message that he somehow had to take care of the women in the family that he perceived as powerful and necessary for his survival. In Susan, he found a needy and powerful woman who would take care of him and allow him to appear role-competent by taking care of her and Lisa. His sexualized relationship with Lisa represented acts of affection, power, control, and revenge. Leon was sexually estranged from Susan and unable to confront her. He was fearful of seeking an adult partner outside of their relationship. He was also aware that Susan had herself been sexually misused at the same age and under the same circumstances as Lisa—and that Susan was hurt by that experience.

It appears that in her relationship with Leon, Susan is symbolically attempting to recapture the love that she was unable to receive as a child. Leon is emotionally immature and sexually passive, as was her father. Susan acted seductively to gain his attention, as she had learned to do in her childhood. Then, when Leon became sexually aroused, she felt betrayed and exploited. Susan then turned to her daughter to meet these pregenital needs. Susan related to Lisa as the maternal grandmother: She demanded that the child take care of her emotionally and projected onto Lisa her anger toward her mother.

Lisa was the "little mother" who often cared for the baby, made family decisions, and attempted to meet her mother's emotional needs, but she was emotionally rejected. She learned to model her mother's behavior to attract Leon's attention. Lisa and Leon became companions and confidants. Leon found, in Lisa, a female who was warm and available and who did not turn away. In sum, the low self-esteem and extreme environmental distrust experienced by Leon and Susan kept them locked into their closed family system, defending themselves against the loss and estrangement they had experienced in their families of origin.

Professionals who come in contact with families who sexually misuse their children may believe that treatment is extremely difficult, if not hopeless. Because of this, many tend to consider the problem solved if the parents separate or if the child victim is removed from the home. In our experience, most families reunite in time; without treatment, the incestuous behavior continues, sometimes with other children. When the family does not reunite, each of the mates often finds similar partners, and the abuse not only continues but multiplies.

## TREATMENT NOTES

The couple in Lisa's family was treated within the interactional framework of the family system at the interpsychic, dyadic, and process level. The therapy was integrative, with an eclectic use of specific techniques.

| Goal 1: Responsibility for Behavior | | |
|---|---|---|
| Specific objectives | Parents will assume responsibility for the incestuous behavior and will admit to the child that she is the victim of poor parenting.<br><br>Defensive behavior will be minimized to open up the closed family system. | |
| Therapeutic interventions | *Reinforce:* | Identity as other than sexually abusive parent; e.g., as homemaker, employee, hobbyist, and so on |
| | *Teach and model:* | Disagreement without power struggle<br>Asking for what one needs<br>Rewarding self<br>Questioning self-defeating assumptions<br>Learning from past experience<br>Owning behavior |
| | *Encourage and support:* | Development of social skills<br>Development of peer relationships<br>Expression of appreciation<br>Self-control |
| | *Give clear feedback:* | On personal strengths, limitations, potential |
| Objective criteria | Leon took responsibility for the incestuous behavior.<br>Susan took responsibility for the poor parenting.<br>Leon's behavior is less withdrawn, and he is beginning to be able to talk about his feelings.<br>Susan's behavior is less placating and childlike.<br>Posture and dress have a less rigid look and appear to express more of the personality of the individuals.<br>Leon and Susan are more assertive in their interactions.<br>The couple's expectations are more optimistic. | |

| Goal 2: Development of Parent-Child Boundaries | | |
|---|---|---|
| Specific objectives | Eliminate role confusion | |
| Therapeutic interventions | *Reinforce:* | Realities of incestuous behavior; e.g., it is a criminal act, harmful to child, anxiety-provoking to parents |
| | *Teach and model:* | Effective parenting |
| | | Separation of sexuality from intimacy |
| | | How to give and receive affection |
| | | Boundary-building vocabulary; e.g., daughter, Dad, Mom, our couple relationship |
| | *Encourage and support:* | Limit setting for self and child |
| | | Awareness of dynamics leading to incestuous behavior |
| | *Environmental manipulation:* | Leon living out of the home during treatment |
| | | Lisa attending nursery school |
| | | Supervision of family by worker other than therapists |
| Objective criteria | The couple is less verbally defensive. | |
| | Leon takes more responsibility for his actions. | |
| | Susan does less "rescuing" of Leon. | |
| | They can express nonsexual nurturing. | |
| | They are less sexually repressive. | |
| | They bowl together regularly. | |

| | Goal 3: Improve Parenting Knowledge and Skills | |
|---|---|---|
| Specific objectives | Understand developmental stages and age-appropriate behavior of children | |
| | Develop skills in limit setting, nurturing, and meeting needs of children | |
| | Experience pleasure and gratification in parenting roles | |
| Therapeutic interventions | *Teach and model:* | Effective parenting techniques |
| | *Encourage and support:* | Participation in parent discussion group at local school |
| | | Learning to play with children |
| | | Allowing child to develop peer relationships |
| Objective criteria | Couple attends parent discussion group regularly. | |
| | Couple demonstrates pleasure in parent role. | |
| | Susan feels closer to her daughter. | |
| | Leon acts less awkward in nonsexual nurturing. | |
| | Lisa exhibits less seductive behavior. | |
| | Lisa greatly improves her relationships with others at school. | |

*Chapter Nine*

---

# Treatment Exercises

"They're looking for recipes" is a statement often made by exasperated educators in the therapy field. We have some. They have been tested and have proven useful in helping people struggling with the myriad problems of sexually abusive family systems. Some are old favorites; others were created spontaneously as the need arose. Our assumption is that these will be used as needed by experienced clinicians and adapted for use with individuals, couples, and groups. Our hope is that they will be refined and modified and that they will engender new ideas and techniques. Interspersed with these exercises are treatment notes—reminders of points mentioned elsewhere in the text. The exercises fall into eight categories:

1. Making contact
2. Ambivalence
3. Putting responsibility where it belongs
4. Getting to feelings
5. Self-image
6. Mastery
7. Sex education
8. Promoting intimacy and communication

# I

## Making Contact

### Note

When presenting any information to the public about the sexual abuse of children, it is essential that some warnings precede the formal presentation. Our statement follows:

> Research suggests that one out of four women have been molested as children. We are beginning to become aware that many males have been molested as children as well. This means that quite a number of you in the audience have had this experience. The material being presented today may stir up some old feelings for you. You may be uncomfortable during this meeting, or you may find that late tonight you have difficulty sleeping. This can be thought of as a positive experience. When you were a child, you did not have the resources to deal with the conflicts you experienced. Now you are an adult (or at least older), and you can deal with these feelings because you are not helpless.
>
> If you or someone you know would like more information or professional services, these are the numbers to call. Would each of you please write these numbers down? Thank you. I'll wait for a minute until everyone has them.

### Awareness of Child Sexual Abuse

This exercise has been used successfully with large community groups to develop a deeper understanding of the complicated factors involved in sexually abusive family systems. We found this especially good with high school students. The exercise nudges people beyond a superficial reaction and encourages them to think more deeply and compassionately about the problem. It is an excellent tool to begin training therapists who will be working in this area.

Form the audience into groups of eight people or less. A minimum of four groups is needed. Give each group one of the following identities:

- Child molestation victims
- Parents who have molested their children
- Spouse of a man or woman who has molested your child
- Professional (instruct this group to use their own profession or one planned in the future, if at all applicable) who is working with a molested child

The leader of the exercise should give the following directions to the groups:

Your task is to have one person begin by completing a sentence that I will give you. Then go around the circle as each member completes the sentence. If you finish before the time is up, use the time in group to discuss the feelings this task brought up for you. The sentences are as follows:

- "I am a molested child, and my greatest concern is. . . ."
- "I am a molesting parent, and my greatest concern is. . . ."
- "My spouse has molested my child, and my greatest concern is. . . ."
- "I am a [teacher, social worker, doctor, police officer], and my greatest concern in working with a sexually abused child is. . . ."

Monitor each group in process to give support and reinforcement, such as: "That's right, we've heard many mothers of victims say exactly that." Also, monitoring provides a closer connection with the audience and enables the facilitator to gauge when it is time to give a three-minute warning and then stop.

Bring groups together and ask generally what some group members would like to share: "Let's start with some of you from the child victim group. Would anyone from this group like to share what came up?" Leaders can use this feedback time to reinforce and comment on what is being said. It has been our experience that the audience comes up with information that would take hours to present in a lecture format. We have found it best not to ask groups to appoint a recorder, since this decreases spontaneity, is time-consuming, and leads to lengthy reports.

-----

## *Rituals for Group*

New kids and adults in ongoing groups worry about how they are going to say what happened, and they wonder what happened to others. Older members are also curious about the newcomer. A ritual is helpful, for it immediately defuses the anxiety, satisfies some curiosity, and helps the newcomer become part of the group. The ritual we use is for old and new members to introduce themselves to the group:

> Hello, my name is _____, and I am here because I [was molested by my grandfather; molested my two daughters; and so on].

Group members can add a sentence or two if they wish. In one of our groups, there was a breakthrough when one girl added that she had been pregnant with her father's child and had had an abortion. A man used the ritual time in an adult group to say that he had been a victim of molestation as a child. Because the ritual procedure is automatic, participants feel less threatened than when they are singled out in a group.

Groups also need a ritual to end each group session. Standing in a circle with arms linked while each group member identifies one thing he or she learned in group or one insight gained or expresses appreciation to one or more group members for their contribution is an effective way to close. This ritual is low risk and offers valuable mutual support.

Celebrating group members' birthdays is a ritual that helps members feel closer to each other. It also helps build self-esteem and feelings of self-worth in the birthday person. Presents are not necessary, but a card or home-baked cake is a meaningful gift.

# Imagery Work

Exercises using imagery are effective in the early phase of treatment because they do not require speakers to talk about their feelings directly. A favorite imagery exercise with our beginning adolescent groups asks speakers to identify the kind of flower, tree, season of the year, or climate they would be if they happened to exist as one of these. After the child identifies, for example, that if she were a flower she would be a daisy, the therapist can ask her what qualities she feels she shares with a daisy.

After all group members have had a chance to identify the kind of flower they are most like, the therapist can ask each one in turn what kind of flowers their parents are. The responses to this question often show that the majority of children consider themselves very different from their parents.

The therapist can then proceed to discuss the degree of compatibility the children feel exists or is lacking between them and their parents.

---

# Note

We have found it important to have food before or after group meetings. Group members do the organizing and arrange for each of the members and the leaders to bring treats. Food is symbolic. It is especially important for needy people. It gives people a way to give, to receive, to nurture, and to be nurtured. Occasionally, we arrange a four-hour marathon group session and have a pot-luck meal.

---

# Animal Fantasy

Animal fantasy is a handy standby that lets people express feelings indirectly. It also reveals diagnostic information during discussion. We have used it individually and in groups and find it especially effective with small children.

Ask the person or group to get as comfortable as possible, to close their eyes, and to think of all the animals they can. Ask them to become aware of the differences, strengths, weaknesses, colors, and sizes. Ask them to think of an animal they would like to be. Then ask them to share. The therapist can promote self-disclosure by statements such as:

- "What is it about the _____ that you like?"
- "How is this similar to you?"
- "The _____ is sometimes quite fierce."
- "Do you ever wish you could _____?"
- "This animal hides in holes. Did you ever want to hide like that?"

## Martian Talk

This is a good icebreaker and sometimes gives the therapist information through the theme of the word selected. Group interactions can be noted, such as who volunteers first. This exercise is popular with teens.

Instruct group members to write their names backwards (for example, Sandy Casey becomes Ydnas Yesac). They can do this first on their own paper and then on a large sheet of paper in front of the group. Ask group members in turn to fantasize that they are Martians, that the words they have made are Martian, and that they are the only ones who know the meaning of the words. Ask each one to use the words in sentences, and have the other group members guess the meaning.

## Note

Resistance is to be respected; it is a measure of the integrity of the character. The functions of resistance are to protect against being overwhelmed, to reduce anxiety, to maintain security, and to cope with unacceptable impulses. The therapist can *join it* by having the person take a stance exaggerating the resistance, *polarize it* by first having the person work with the negative part that is blocking therapeutic progress and then with the part the person wants to explore, or *confront it* by having the person explore the function served by the resistance. Resistance is to be respected and worked with, not broken through.

## Magic Box

The magic box is another oldie but goodie. It works well with children, individually or in groups, by helping them think about what they value.

Tell the person or group about a magic box that can make itself very big or very small. Explain that part of its magic is that it can contain anything the group member wants it to: "If you came into this room and found the magic box waiting for you to open it, what would be in it? It could be something real or some kind of power. What would it be?"

## Pick a Family

Ask adolescents: "What families on television shows would you want your family to be like? What is it about the TV family that you like? What are the differences between your family and your favorite TV family?" This exercise helps adolescents define the things that have to change in their family for the family to be more appropriate, less dysfunctional, and happier.

## II

# Ambivalence

## Ambivalence Is OK

All family members are blocked in expressing themselves until they have found an acceptable way to state their ambivalent feelings. It is extremely helpful for the therapist to take the lead and to make it permissible to feel several feelings at once. Also, it is useful to separate feelings toward a person from feelings about their behavior. We explain the following:

- It's OK to love the person and to hate a specific behavior.
- It's OK to appreciate yourself as a person and not like something you have done.
- It's OK to hate a parent. (Some kids and adults working on old traumas need this permission.)
- It's OK to have feelings change toward a person.

---

## "How I'm Feeling about _____ Today" Charts

This teaches the concept of a continuum. Many people in the families we have worked with tend to polarize. Things are either good or bad, black or white; you either love or hate a person. The charts are permission-giving. They also demonstrate that group members will have different feelings. This is especially useful with open-ended groups, for one member may be expressing rage toward a family member while another person may need to protect that person. Without the chart, we found members blocked because they believed that their feelings of rage or protection would be disapproved of or would frighten other group members.

Have the group design the charts. Ask what is the most positive feeling that, for example, a girl can have toward her father (the molesting parent). What is the most negative? The leader draws the continuum, explaining: "Sometimes we feel closer to the negative feelings, sometimes we feel closer to the positive feelings, and sometimes we are in the middle." Large papers and felt pens can be used; however, we have found that a metal chart with movable magnetic markers is best. This way, the chart can be available for each meeting. Before group, members can move their markers, if they wish, to indicate changes in feelings. This can then be addressed during group. Charts can be used in adult groups as well, for self and for spouse. Examples of charts we have used follow.

---

### The Molesting Person

| Castrate him; put him in jail | | | | | Run away with him and be his lover |
|---|---|---|---|---|---|
| 1 | 2 | 3 | 4 | 5 | 6 |
| Sandy | Marianne | Jane | Ruth | | Kathy |

### The Silent Partner

| She should drop dead | | | | | I only feel strong love |
|---|---|---|---|---|---|
| 1 | 2 | 3 | 4 | 5 | 6 |
| Kathy Marianne | Ruth | Jane | | Sandy | |

### Myself

| I think about hurting myself | | | | | I think I'm GREAT |
|---|---|---|---|---|---|
| 1 | 2 | 3 | 4 | 5 | 6 |
| | Kathy | Jane | Ruth | Marianne Sandy | |

# III

## Putting Responsibility Where It Belongs

### Tricking Yourself

Our treatment program will not allow an offending parent to be part of the treatment program unless he can say, "I molested my child." Initially, their statements contain buts: "but I was drinking"; "but she wanted me to." A major goal of treatment is for the molesting parent to take full responsibility for the sexual abuse. An effective approach we have found to open the person's psychodynamics and move away from rationalization is for the leader to say the following:

> I know I shouldn't overeat, but I find ways to trick myself so that I can do it. I might say that I won't eat so much the next day, or that I'll do exercises, or that it's not really fattening. We all have ways to trick ourselves. What did you say to yourself? *How did you trick yourself to make molesting your child OK?*

### The Diabetic Child

This analogy has helped kids, their parents, and professionals in training to understand that an adult committing molestation acts is always responsible, regardless of the child's behavior. This has also been a very effective lead-in to discussion of the victim's pleasure response. Everyone can quickly grasp how the child in the analogy would find some enjoyment and still not be responsible for what is happening. Many adult women who had been victimized as children have heard this analogy and gained tremendous relief from the insight they experienced.

The group leader tells the following story:

> The doctor told the parents of a child that she must not have sweets. He told them that because she had diabetes, sweets would be very harmful

to her. Both parents understood this and tried to explain it to their little girl.

One day, the mother went shopping, and the father called the child into his room. He knew it was not OK, but he did it anyway. He gave her a candy bar. She was very happy. He told her that she must not tell anyone, especially her mother, because she'd get very upset.

Whenever the little girl was alone with her father, she'd beg him for candy. She liked the candy. She liked her special secret with Dad.

Everyone became upset when they found out that the father was giving his little girl candy secretly. The doctor and the mother were very angry. The father said: "I was just giving her what she wanted. Sometimes she asked for it. And besides, she enjoyed it."

The leader then asks the group, "What do you think?" The leader can play the father's advocate to elicit a strong response by saying: "But she liked it! Wasn't he being a good father, just trying to make her happy?"

Offenders, spouses who are protecting offenders, and some professionals dealing with children have difficulty defending their "seductive child" stance after hearing this analogy.

---

# Note

Do not be intimidated by young people in group sessions who loudly lament, "This is boring!" Life is boring for them much of the time.

---

# Skit: "Dad Hit Me with the Car"

We found this skit needed at least two and a half hours to have group members fully explore all the feelings and insights generated. The use of "feeling" cards has interesting potential for research. We have used this skit to train police officers and mental health professionals, to teach high school students, and to provide treatment to our child victim groups.

1. Make a packet of large index cards (5-inch by 8-inch) for each person participating in the group. Mark each card in large letters. More than six or seven cards is unwieldy. We use "anger," "shame," "confusion," "happy," "sadness," and "relief" on cards and leave one blank to enable each person to state a feeling that might not be on a card.
2. Next make cards for the cast of characters. We use manila folders cut in half. In very large letters on the front, write the character's name. On the back, write the dialogue for each character, note who is to start, and number the cards.

The skit is done with two leaders: one is the child, the other is the cast of characters. Stop after each of the characters speaks, and ask group members to hold up the card or cards that express what they believe the child in the skit is feeling. Take time to let each person comment. If this is done in a therapy session, it is common to find that someone will also begin to go into their own feelings when a similar situation happened to them. We have found it best to use the time to explore the spontaneous disclosure. The power of the group to support a member's feelings indirectly by using the feeling cards is truly amazing. Because of the variety of responses, this technique helps to clarify and make ambivalence OK. Young people have asked that we repeat this skit at subsequent meetings. It has been one of our most effective tools.

| *Child* | *Cast of Characters* |
| --- | --- |
| *Introduction:* I'm fourteen years old, and I'm having a lot of trouble now. When I was just nine, I began to get molested. It's easier to explain if I tell my story as if I were hit by a car. | *Make screeching sounds of brakes; then a crash. As Dad:* That didn't hurt did it? |
| *To Dad:* No, just shaken. Do you love me? | |
| *To sister:* Dad hit me with the car, and I'm afraid he'll do it | *As sister:* Boy, Mom will really get upset if you do |

again. Do you think I should tell Mom?

*To best friend:* I want to tell you a secret. Promise you won't tell anybody? My dad hit me with a car.

*To Mom:* I don't know how to tell you. . . . Dad hit me with a car.

*To teacher:* It's kind of hard for me to tell you.

*To teacher:* Dad hit me with the car.

that. [*Pause*] He probably won't do it again. Anyway, he can't help it when he's drinking. Besides, he didn't mean it.

*As best friend:* My God, how gross! He did that to you? He hit you with a car? How could anyone do that? My dad wouldn't do that to me!

*As Mom:* Oh, that's terrible. Your father wouldn't do anything like that! Are you sure you're telling the truth? [*Pause*] You must tell the truth now, because he could get into all kinds of trouble. He might lose his job.

*As teacher:* You're acting really strange. Is there anything wrong?

*As teacher:* That's OK, you can tell me.

*As teacher:* Shhh! We'll talk about it later. [*Pause*] Well, if he really did that, we'll have to tell someone.

*As police officer:* [*Stands over child, keeps pacing and writing, talks over child's attempts to respond, doesn't give her a chance to answer*] I know this is hard for you, but I have to ask you some questions. When did this happen? Has this happened before? Did anyone see this happen? Why didn't you tell someone sooner? Did he hit you with his bumper or with his fender? Did he say anything while he was hitting you or immediately after?

*To police officer:* [*Tries to respond, but officer talks over every attempt*]

*As Dad:* You know this is all your fault! Look at all the trouble you're causing!

*To Dad:* [*Looks ashamed*]

*As Dad:* [*To police officer*] But she asked for it! She wanted to get hit. I could tell by the way she was walking. [*Pause*] I was just teaching her to be careful.

*To audience:* Maybe it was my fault? Maybe I shouldn't have told.

The leader should stop each time there is a character change and have the group display the appropriate feeling cards. Do this again at the end of the skit.

---

# Soap Opera

We have used this special psychodrama with our girls' group, ages nine to twelve. Gather an assortment of men's and women's clothing, including hats and wigs—the more outrageous, the better.

Pile all this in the middle of the floor and give the following instructions:

> You will have fifteen minutes while we are out of the room to create a soap opera to entertain your leaders. It's probably a good idea to choose a director. We'll return for the show.

When we used this exercise, it not only was fun for the kids and the leaders but also revealed helpful diagnostic information. Part of the drama presented related to an incest problem, although this was not mentioned in the instructions.

_____

# Big Mama

"Big Mama" was a huge doll made from a king-size pillow. A cord, tied part way down the pillow, created a head. Two pairs of stuffed panty hose were tied on to make arms and legs. Big Mama was dressed in female adult clothing, and she wore a wig. Her wonderful wraparound arms were great for nurturing in psychodramas. We used her in many ways. For example, group members were asked to draw a face that represented their mother's face. Then each member, one at a time, pinned her drawing on the blank face of Big Mama. The group member then addressed the doll, telling her all that she wished she could tell her real Mom. She then asked for what she needed from Big Mama.

Much time is needed for this exercise. Big Mama can be used equally well with adults.

_____

# IV

## Getting to Feelings

### Note

We have found it best not to have a real person portray Mother or Father during psychodramas. When the person working has very strong, often volatile feelings, having to address a real person blocks the expression of those feelings. Whenever the therapist or a group member is involved in a role play or psychodrama with a person who is working on something, it is important to "de-role." One may say, for example, "I am no longer your mother."

### Confronting a Feeling

This works well with individuals and can be used within couple and group settings as well. Ask the person if she or he is willing to try an experiment to work on a predominant feeling. If the person (in this case, a female child), is willing, proceed as follows:

1. Have her close her eyes and relax. (If much tension is evident, begin with a relaxation exercise.)
2. Have her select a feeling that she wants to explore further.
3. Instruct her to allow a mental image that represents the feeling to emerge. This could be an object, a fantasy creature, and so on. Ask her to get a clear picture of this image and become aware of what her feelings are toward it.
4. Let her talk with the image, and follow the dialogue through to its conclusion.
5. During the exercise thus far, the person is not discussing what is going on for her. She is following directions, guided by the therapist. The therapist should observe changes in breathing, skin coloration, and body movement during the process.

6. If she wishes, the person can share what happened during the process with the therapist.

---

# Opening

This is another exercise to work with a predominant feeling. (Again, we are assuming that the person is female, though the exercise works equally well for males.)

1. Have person relax and close her eyes. (If much tension is evident, begin with a relaxation exercise.)
2. Say: "Imagine that you are in a garden. [*Pause*] Picture a wall around the garden. [*Pause*] There is a gate in the wall. Moving closer, you'll notice your name on the gate, and written below it is the name of the feeling you want to work on."
3. Ask her to experience herself face to face with the feeling. Tell her that when she is ready, she is to open the gate.
4. The therapist can then work with the visualization or the person's difficulty with opening the gate.

---

# Vaginal Appreciation

The vaginal appreciation exercise developed when leaders became aware of the extremely negative image that the girls in a group had of their bodies. It has also been used in an adult women's group. It needs to be done with a sense of fun and high energy. It has evangelical overtones and needs the second leader to respond and encourage group response. This is a great place for leaders to indulge any tendency to overact.

> Did you know that more than half the people in the world have vaginas?
> Did you know that Suzanne Sommers has a vagina? Jackie Kennedy? Indira Gandhi? Nancy Reagan?
> Your great and wonderful leader, _____ _____, has a vagina!

And do you know why?

Because they're women!

What good are vaginas? That's how babies get out! They stretch (a prop made of something stretchy here is great).

They are also good for sex. Oh, yes. Sex. When you want it.

Vaginas are good because they are passageways to let out menstrual blood. A vagina's great for holding tampons.

Women's genitals are marvelous! Every woman has the same parts—like all faces have noses, eyes, mouths—and yet each has its own special look, just like faces. [*Illustrate quickly with felt pen on large paper*] Look, there's even a part that's just for pleasure: the clitoris.

Isn't that great?!

Let's hear some appreciation: Yea!

> Give me a *V*!
> Give me an *A*!
> Give me a *G*!
> Give me an *I*!
> Give me an *N*!
> Give me an *A*!
> What have you got?
> Yea!!

---

# Gross Out

This technique has been used spontaneously from time to time to desensitize and to give a young person permission to tell about what has happened to her sexually. This also lets group members know that the leader has heard everything and will not be shocked, disgusted, or have bad feelings toward the person involved in the sexual activity. The leader universalizes the sort of sexual goings-on that have happened to others. The tone is light. The leader continues the soliloquy despite the groans and protestations of group members. Meanwhile, the second leader plays it straight and tells the group something like: "I don't know how to get her to stop. She just goes on like this every once in a while." The first leader uses the energy and the humor of the adolescents. We get more bizarre and creative every time we do this. An example follows:

It's really hard to understand why some people do sexual things. I mean, I've heard of people who will put their penis between someone's toes or under their arm. It's *really* gross if they come in your hair—sticky stuff all over. I mean, it must be really hard to wash out. It's probably a good thing that semen doesn't come in all different colors. Then if it's in your mouth and he comes, stuff comes out your nose sometimes, maybe even your ears. No, I don't think it would come out your ears. Maybe some men would even put a penis in someone's ear. Eh? What's that? I can't hear you. I mean, how could someone talk about that kind of stuff with another person?

After one of these "gross outs," three young girls, one of whom had been in therapy for a year, described incidents that they had been too ashamed to mention. We have known group members to refer playfully to this exercise at a later time.

---

# Expressing the Opposite

People who are blocked from expressing a feeling are often helped by being asked to act out an exaggeration of the opposite feeling. Have them role play, exaggerating as much as possible, how much they really love their partner's withdrawal behavior, how much they appreciate the sense of frustration, how they experience it in their bodies, and so on. This helps to release the block.

---

# Note

We believe that it is essential to go through a specific process before initiating therapeutic exercises such as role playing, self-dialogue, body work, and psychomotor techniques. The steps are as follows:

1. Ask, "Would you be willing to try an experiment?"
2. If the response is yes, proceed.
3. If the response is a question, respond with, "I'd like to have you

trust me and commit yourself without knowing, just yet, what's going to happen."

4. If the response is no, drop it, saying, "I respect that."

Do not intellectualize with a person who is resistant to trying an action method. It has to be done, not discussed. Just drop it and go on to something else.

---

## Add Variety to a Group

Dyads:

We have found it useful in groups to break up into dyads for a short time (ten to fifteen minutes) and then come together as a group to share experiences.

Separate Groups:

Watch the energy level rise on this one! Have the group divide into a male group and a female group for half the session. Fruitful discussion follows about how and why this is a positive or negative experience. Lots to explore here.

Film:

Showing the film *Incest: The Victim No One Believes* generates a great deal of material to work on in both child and adult groups. Many insights have been gained.

Marathon:

Adding an occasional four-hour session to a group that normally meets for an hour and a half has been effective in getting to deeper feelings.

Activities:

An occasional field trip for swimming, roller skating, and so on with the children's and the teenager's groups has helped to increase social skills with peers, develop group cohesiveness, encourage bonding with the leaders, provide diagnostic information, and provide a fun break.

---

# Guest Speakers

We have invited the following guest speakers to our adolescent groups:

1. An adult woman who was molested by a family member as a child and appears to have successfully coped with her experience. She spoke openly of her feelings then and now. She discussed what has happened to her. She told of her present satisfying life and invited questions. There was a very positive group response. Actually getting to know someone who has been there and made it through was a valuable experience for the girls. The woman's name was brought up again and again in subsequent groups.
2. Two deputy district attorneys came to answer the girls' questions, to provide an opportunity for the girls to ventilate their feelings about the court process and legal system, and to learn from the girls what could be changed to help the child victim. Feelings of self-esteem and mastery were definitely enhanced as a result of this meeting.
3. Sex educators came equipped with films, rubber models, contraceptive devices, and so on. It is essential that the leaders preview their presentation or interview them privately in advance. The educator must be able to relate well with teens and not be revolted by what has happened to them. The teens will interpret negative reactions toward the offense or the offender as the person's (and the public's) attitude toward them as well. With the power of the group setting behind them, the teens will test the sex educator. Count on it! They know that you, the therapists, think they are OK, but you are paid to be helpful. If you are unable to find someone suitable, borrow their material and do it yourself.

---

# Note

Our procedure is to have an individual session with a child before he or she enters group. Our objectives are as follows:

1. To evaluate the child for group membership.
2. To provide the child with information regarding the group's purpose, rules, activities, and so on.
3. To get acquainted with the child and to relieve some of the stress related to entering a group of this nature.

After obtaining the child's permission, we have a group member call the child before the first meeting and talk. This does good things for both of them.

A careful explanation of confidentiality must be given to the child. We tell them that we have one exception to the confidentiality rule: If a child tells about other incidents of abuse, we will report this to the appropriate authorities so that the child can be protected. We have had children in therapy "slip" and tell about severely abusive incidents. This was their way of seeking help while still appearing not to have betrayed the family.

It is essential to discuss this confidentiality issue with the child's parents or guardians and with the social worker. They must not press the child for information about what happens in group. Skillful diplomacy is required because the adults often perceive this as a threatening shift of power.

# V

## Self-Image

### I Like Myself

An old standby, good for everyone, is to have people say:

I like myself because. . . .

Individuals who are part of a sexually abusive family system often cannot come up with any response—and you work with that.

---

### Fantasies

Ask family members, "What do you fantasize for yourself two years, five years, and ten years from today?" This directs their attention toward goals and is also an opportunity to look at their self-image. How did each person decide? What is it about the life-style that is appealing? How do they get from where they are to where they want to be?

---

### Advantages and Disadvantages of Being Male or Female

This exercise is useful in working with a couples group. With members of the same sex, it clarifies feelings and perceptions about members of the other sex. It helps them to talk about what it is like to be a man or a woman in our society in front of members of the other sex, without fear of being challenged.

The couples group is divided into a male group and a female group. Each is given a large sheet of paper and a felt pen. The paper is divided by a line down the center. One side of the paper is titled "The Advantages of Being _____"; the other side is titled "The Disadvantages of Being _____." The male group is told to write *Female* on both sides of the sheet, and the female group is told to write *Male*. The two groups meet separately for twenty minutes and complete their lists. The groups then exchange lists. Discuss, in the same-sex group, how members feel about the perceptions of the other sex. Where do they agree? Where do they disagree? Bring both groups together and discuss feelings generated by the lists. Give each sex group uninterrupted time to express their feelings.

This works well during the restructure phase of treatment. If attempted when there is still a lot of unresolved hostility in the group, it may not be effective.

_____

# Note

Mastery and self-esteem are increased when a person helps others and develops skills. These developments must be nurtured, promoted, and celebrated. We create quite a bit of hoopla over someone asking for a raise, getting a job, obtaining a driver's license, learning to roller skate, completing a difficult school assignment, and so on.

_____

# VI

## Mastery

### Disengaging from Old Traumas

Therapy with sexually abusive family systems involves high drama. Intense emotions have often not been expressed for survival reasons. Both adult partners in the couple relationship often have histories of being abused as children in their own families of origin. It is not enough to have a person emote. A sense of closure and mastery is also needed.

The following process separates painful, constricting past association from the present and helps a person to look at life decisions that can be changed in the here and now. This is especially effective in individual therapy with adults (in the following example, with a man).

1. Have the person relax as much as possible, and say: "In a few minutes, you will again see the scene that has been so painful for you. When this event occurred, you did not have the resources to deal with it."
2. Tell the person that you are going to take his hand. Hold his hand and say: "You now have the resources right in your hand to deal with this event. When you need to use your resources, squeeze my hand." The touch of the hand is reassuring and dissipates anxiety.
3. Explain that the "now" person, who has his resources in his hand, will be able to look at what happened to the "then" person involved in the painful situation. The objective is not to reexperience the feelings but rather to detach from them. Simply have the person look back and squeeze when he needs to.
4. As the exercise comes to a close, have the now person give the then person what he needed to deal with the trauma.

# Reparenting Exercise

Adults working on past difficulties with parenting experiences cannot "destroy" a parent symbolically in therapy without also destroying the person who nourished them. This exercise separates the positive parent from the negative parent.

The person working (a man, in this example) chooses from the people in the group two positive parents and two negative parents. Even if he grew up in a single-parent home, he will have things to say to the absent parent.

First he works with the negative parents. He tells them exactly what to say to him, and he responds to them with statements that he was unable to make in the past. It is important that his directions be followed exactly by the role-playing parents. The therapist can give the person suggestions and can guide him but must leave him in control. Creative diversions by those playing the roles will distract. Trust that the working person knows what he needs to hear and have happen. For example:

*Negative father:*   You are a Mama's boy. I think you are disgusting.

*Negative mother:*   John, why do you say those things to him? You know he can't help being the way he is. Adam tries to please you, too.

*Adam:*   I'm sick of hearing you put me down, Dad. Shut up and leave me alone. And you, Mom, you bitch! You never protected me. You just whined. I hate you!

Adam stops for a moment, tells his negative parents what to say, and continues. The therapist guides and encourages until Adam feels finished. They then move on to the positive parents. The therapist prefaces this part of the work by saying that positive parenting includes nurturing, supporting, protecting, and limit setting. Adam, with guidance from the therapist if needed, incorporates each of these areas in his interactions with his positive parents.

*Positive father:*   I appreciate your special qualities. You are a fine, sensitive boy.

|              |                                                                                                                          |
| ------------:| ------------------------------------------------------------------------------------------------------------------------ |
| *Adam:*          | Thank you, Dad. Would you and Mom sit closer together? |
| *Positive mother:* | I love you very much, Adam. |
| *Adam:*          | [*Pause*] Would you hold me? I just want to be quiet for a while. |
| *Positive father:* | Adam, it is not your job to take care of the relationship between your mother and me. We are adults, and we can take care of ourselves. |
| *Positive mother:* | It's our job to take care of you. We love you and enjoy caring for you. |
| *Positive father:* | I want you to know that I am an adult and can handle your feelings. You can be as angry as you want or as tender or as sad. I will not be hurt or swayed when I set limits. I love you, and I will set limits for you. |

---

# *Courtroom*

This exercise has been used primarily to prepare children for testifying in court. It is made clear to all that this is not a rehearsal, since the procedures can and do become quite creative. It helps children gain a sense of mastery and is useful for those who have been through the criminal court process to express leftover feelings about their experiences. Children in groups have asked again and again for the courtroom exercise. Often, the "judge" will tell the "offender" and the "mother" what the child has difficulty expressing.

To begin, one leader gives the following directions: "Let's play 'Courtroom' because Cindy has to go to court in two weeks to testify. The leaders will be the jury. What other roles do we have?" Get responses from the group that include judge, district attorney, offender, the offender's attorney, social worker, court reporter, mother, and witnesses, if there are enough people. Sometimes we have used a doll to play the offender because no one in the group wanted that part. At other times, a child has asked to play the offender, most often using the role to tell the child victim all the feelings of remorse and responsibility she wishes had been said to her. Many times the action stops as group members get in touch with and work through feelings.

---

# Situation Game

This exercise works well with adolescent groups to develop mastery.

### Materials Needed

- A stack of index cards, each stating a situation that requires a problem-solving response
- Two pads of large paper
- Felt pens
- A timer with alarm

### Directions

Divide group into two teams. Both teams listen to the leader read a situation card aloud. Each team writes as many solutions to the problem situation as they can think of. When the alarm goes off (in two minutes), the team with the most responses on their paper wins.

### Sample Situation Cards

- Your little sister has just told the kids in the neighborhood about the sexual molestation in the family. This really cute guy you haven't dated yet but would like to says: "Your sister is making up terrible stories about your family." What do you do now?
- You (a male) are visiting a friend for the evening. While your friend is in his room talking on the phone, you go into the kitchen. Your friend's mother is sitting at the table drinking beer. She looks very attractive. She asks you to come over to her and scratch her back. Now what do you do?

---

# Problem Solving and Rehearsing

Many difficult situations arising from molestation behavior are addressed in therapy by using the following procedure (with a girl victim, in this example):

1. The person working states the situation that is causing difficulty for her.
2. She explores why this is a problem for her.
3. With a felt pen on a large sheet of paper, she writes all the solutions she can think of. If this takes place in a group setting, others can add to the list. This should be regarded as a brainstorming session—all ideas are accepted, regardless of feasibility.
4. She reviews the list and checks those solutions that best suit her.
5. From the checked solutions, she chooses one possibility.
6. She rehearses the chosen solution through role play.
7. She follows through with the solution outside the group.
8. She reports the results of her action to the therapist or group. Success is celebrated. If the solution does not work, other alternatives from the list are reviewed and another is selected.

Rehearsal is an essential part of this process. We role play the situation until the person develops a feeling of confidence. Some of the situations we have worked with using this technique are the following:

- Responding to kids at school who know about the molestation and tease the child victim or ask questions that the child does not want to answer.
- Telling extended family members about the molestation before they read about it in the newspaper.
- Responding to friends about where the child has been after she's returned from spending two weeks in the children's shelter.
- A boy who has been molested needing to explain to his gym teacher that he becomes extremely uncomfortable when he must engage in contact sports with other guys, especially wrestling.
- Explaining to friends why a spouse is not living at home any longer.

# *Your Body Belongs to You*

This learning exercise is essential for child victims in therapy and is useful for parents and school personnel as part of safety education for a child. The following is an example of how you can teach the child that sex between adults and children is not acceptable, that it is appropriate for a child to say no to an adult under certain circumstances, what a child should do if faced with a sexual molestation situation, and what will happen when the child tells about an incident. The following example should be modified according to the age of the children being addressed.

We've all learned to do things to take care of our bodies. What are some of those things? [*Brushing teeth, exercising, and so on. If in a classroom or group therapy room, it's helpful to list responses.*]

Who owns your body? [*Allow time for responses.*]

Your body belongs to you. You own your body. We know we need to take care of our bodies. One way we take care of ourselves is by not letting people hurt us or touch our bodies in ways that make us very uncomfortable. Let's talk about touching. What are some ways that people touch you that make you feel good? [*Responses may include hugging, tickling, wrestling, kissing, and holding hands.*] What are some of the ways that people touch you that don't feel good? [*Responses may include hitting, kicking, and rubbing whiskers on your face.*] When can some of these things [*point to list*] not feel good or make you feel uncomfortable? [*Responses may include a relative that makes you kiss him even though he's got bad breath, hugging too tight, tickling when you want it to stop, and so on.*]

So sometimes touching is OK and makes us feel good, and sometimes touching is not OK and doesn't make us feel good. Since your body belongs to you, it's OK to say no or to tell someone to stop if they touch you in a way that makes you uncomfortable.

There are parts of your body that it's not OK for a grown-up person to touch. And it's not OK for a grown-up person to ask you to touch his body or her body in those places. Those places are the penis, the buttocks, between a girl's legs where the vagina is, or on the breast area of a girl. [*With young children, touch those places on yourself to illustrate.*] If a grown-up person touches you in those places or asks you to touch his body in those places, you should say no or tell him to stop. Your body belongs to you. It's not OK for a grown-up to touch a child in those places.

Check for understanding at this point, and then take time to discuss the exception of a physical examination by a medical person with a parent present. Then say:

If a grown-up touches you [*review places*], there are two things you must do:

1. Say "Stop!" or "No!"
2. Tell_____.

If a parent is talking to his or her child, add: "And I want you to know that I will see that the behavior stops, because it's my job to protect you. I will not be angry with you for whatever happened."
Test learning here by asking:

- Suppose the grown-up person that did this was someone you liked a lot, what would you do? (Stay with this until correct response is given.)
- Suppose the grown-up was a police officer?
- Suppose the grown-up offered you $5.00?

Then respond:

- That's right: because your body belongs to you.

---

## Body Work: Defiance

This exercise helps a person to own personal power. In a physical way, it moves a person from a helpless, nonassertive, victim stance to a feeling of control. The exercise can be used in individual, couple, or group sessions.
Have a boy, for example, stand with his arms raised to the shoulders, elbows bent. He is to stand about two feet in front of another person. Looking directly at the other person, he is to say loudly and repeatedly: "Get out! Get out of my way!"
As he does this, he makes strong, thrusting gestures by putting a raised elbow in front of him at shoulder level and pulling back

hard, following with the other elbow. There is no physical contact—just gestures. The other person does not respond but maintains eye contact. Have the pair switch roles after a few minutes. Follow with discussion questions such as: "What was it like for you to be defiant? What feelings were brought up?" Repeat the exercise.

A variation is to have all group members walk around the room shouting and gesturing; then discuss the exercise with the group, sharing feelings. Other variations are to growl, hiss, claw like a cat, stick out one's jaw, and so on.

---

# Practicing Self-Protection

Role-playing situations that arouse confusion or helplessness in children are effective in helping them feel less vulnerable to future exploitation. A situation commonly identified by victims as highly threatening is one in which the molesting parent attempts to molest again.

The therapist asks for two volunteers to role play this situation. One child is designated to play the molesting parent; the other child plays the victim. The child assuming the victim role is directed by the therapist to play the part the way she actually would behave in order to prevent being molested. The other group members can coach both players during the role play interaction.

When the role play is over, the players should discuss their feelings during the exercise. The other group members should be asked to comment and make suggestions.

Each group member should have the opportunity to role play the part of the potential victim. Because assertiveness training requires repeated experience in being assertive, this exercise is valuable in all phases of treatment.

---

# VII

## Sex Education

### Parts List

This exercise is often used to desensitize and educate professionals in training. We have found that it also has therapeutic value when used in a group therapy setting. It not only desensitizes the group and lessens embarrassment but also gives permission for a variety of terms to be used. The tone is light; the mood shifts quickly from embarrassment to good humor. The exercise often produces surprises, since people come up with terms from their childhood or colloquial expressions. It's a great lead-in to discussions of body image.

The leader directs the discussion, using large paper and felt pens to make a list that the group can see: "There are lots of terms used to refer to female genitals." (The exercise goes on to male genitals later; usually each takes a full therapy session.) "I think it would be helpful for us to list as many as we can think of. Perhaps we will learn some new terms. OK, who's going to be the first brave one to come up with a name or expression?"

When all the words are listed, follow up by asking: "What words are you most comfortable using in group? Do any words stir up strong feelings? Why?"*

### Note

Adults as well as children benefit from sex education sessions. In some instances, we have had adults play sex education games and take part in very basic presentations of human sexuality. This was

---

*In a girls' victim group, no word for female genitals was acceptable. The girls stated that all the words were disgusting, including medical (anatomical) terms.

done to keep them informed of what their children were learning and was a nonthreatening way to present basics. Also, we have had guest speakers, films, and discussions specifically for adults.

Both adults and children appreciate having an Anonymous Box. This box, passed around the group, gives members the opportunity to put in a slip of paper on which they have written a question or comment related to the discussion. The leader and group members then respond to each question or comment.

---

# *Definition Game*

This game has been played numerous times in group by children and by adults. It is a learning tool and assists in removing the overwhelming shame most members in sexually abusive families experience when discussing sexual issues.

## Materials Needed

- Two bulb-type bicycle horns.
- Index cards, each with a word relating to sexuality (*vulva, condom, mini-pad, herpes,* and so on) and the definition of the word.
- Large paper and felt pen to keep score.

## Directions

1. Form two teams with three people on each team. (It adds to the fun if teams have names.)
2. Designate a scorekeeper and a leader to read the words. The rest of the group members are judges.
3. The leader reads each word aloud. The first team to honk the team horn gets to give a definition. If the judges decide they are correct, they win ten points. If they are wrong, they lose ten points, and then the other team has a chance to define the word without a penalty.
4. The team with the highest score is given prizes, usually food treats.

---

## *Triad Discussions of Sexual Topics*

We have found that sexual topics are more easily discussed in three-person groups. A small group is a safe place to become desensitized, to acknowledge ignorance, and so on.

We divide the group into triads and give each triad a stack of index cards. Each card has one word on it relating to sexuality (for example, *breast, orgasm, masturbation, menstruation, intercourse,* and so on). The cards are spread out face down. One person begins by selecting a card and talking about the subject or an issue around the subject for one minute. Then the next person selects a card and talks for one minute. After all three group members have had a turn, they take three minutes to discuss their feelings and to make comments. Then it is time for another round. A leader using a gong to keep time can add to the fun of this learning experience.

# VIII

## Promoting Intimacy and Communication

### Dealing with Negative Feelings

Teaching couples and families to deal with negative feelings begins with the recognition that:

1. Conflict in an intimate relationship is inevitable.
2. Not dealing with a conflict creates stress in the relationship.
3. A conflict dealt with dysfunctionally creates alienation in the relationship.
4. A conflict dealt with constructively can strengthen the relationship.

Two methods that we have taught and have had couples practice in the treatment setting follow:

#### Outside Carry-over

In this situation, one partner is angry about something outside the relationship, and the negative feelings are likely to affect interactions with the partner. The angry partner states clearly where the anger belongs, states that it would be helpful to get the feelings expressed, and asks the partner if he or she would be willing to listen. The angry partner then:

1. Requests an appointment with the partner.
2. Tells what is bothering him or her. (Partner is to listen sympathetically, interrupt as little as possible, and refrain from giving advice.)
3. Expresses appreciation to partner for listening and sharing.

A sample dialogue follows:

*She:* I'm angry about what happened at the office today. May I talk about it?

He:     I want to hear about it, but I've got a phone call I'd like to make right now. Can you wait until I've finished?

She:    OK.

        [*Later*]

He:     I'm ready to listen now, OK?

She:    OK. I'm so angry with those people at work. It seems that since we've got the word processor, they've become really careless about the reports they give me to do.

He:     That sounds frustrating. Tell me more. [*Rather than "That's to be expected."*]

She:    Well, for instance, John revised a report three times today. It seems like all he thinks about is the machine. He doesn't consider how much work it is for me. We *got* the machine because I was overloaded!

He:     Seems pretty inconsiderate. [*Rather than "You should. . . ." or "Couldn't you. . . ."*]

She:    Darn right it is! I had three people waiting for me to finish reports at 4:00 today. I felt like I was just part of the machine. I know I need to do something, but right now I'm so angry, it's really difficult.

He:     You're really having a hard time. [*Rather than "I know, because I used to. . . ."*]

She:    It's just been a rotten day today. I fumed all the way home and almost went through a red light.

He:     That's upsetting. [*Rather than "You need to be careful" or "My day's been awful too."*]

She:    It sure is. Thanks for listening. This really helps me.

He:     I'm glad. Do you want anything?

She:    No. Thanks for asking.


## Sandbagging

In this situation, one partner is angry about something the other has done. The angry partner (in this example, the man) wants to get rid of the feeling but does not want to start a long fight. He states that he has an angry feeling that he has been holding on to, makes an appointment with his partner, and talks about it. The partner can sympathize, apologize, or just listen.

*He:*   I've been sandbagging some angry feelings since yesterday, and I'd like to tell you about it. Can you take it now?

*She:*  I'm ready to listen.

*He:*   I didn't like it when you were joking with my mother at dinner about my leaving clothes around the bedroom. I felt put down and not respected.

*She:*  I hear you. [*Rather than "But you did leave your. . . ." or "We really didn't mean. . . ."*]

      Now I have some sandbagged feelings for you. Can you take it?

*He:*   It sounds like you want to get back at me right now. I'd like to wait a while. If you still want to after the children are in bed, I'll be ready to listen then.

      [*Later*]

*She:*  I'm ready to talk about some angry feelings I've been holding on to. Are you ready now?

*He:*   I'm ready to listen.

*She:*  I was angry yesterday because you invited your mother for dinner and didn't let me know. All I had was those dumb leftovers. I felt like you didn't consider my feelings, and I was embarrassed because your mother is such a good cook and I had to serve that casserole.

*He:*   I hear you. [*Rather than "Now you tell me" or "The casserole was fine."*]

---

## Ideal Partner

In couple relationships, the therapist often finds that partners have difficulty asking for what they want or telling what they are willing to give. Needs are sometimes expressed or perceived as demands, and a power struggle begins. Or one partner will give something with the expectation that she or he will get something in return that has not been stated. Often, partners think, "If you love me, you will know what my needs are and will meet them."

This exercise helps partners to clarify needs and to state which needs a partner wishes to meet. A partner's need is a request, and a need met is a gift, not a response to a demand.

We ask each person to take a turn at being the Ideal Partner. One partner tells the Ideal Partner what to say. The Ideal Partner then repeats those things exactly. For example:

> *Partner:* I want you, Ideal Partner, to tell me that I don't have to be strong—that it's OK to show you my weaknesses.
>
> *Ideal Partner:* It's OK to be weak.
>
> *Therapist:* John, from the look on your face, I have a hunch that the statement doesn't quite fit. Is there some other way your Ideal Partner can state that?
>
> *Partner:* Yes, that's not quite right. Let's try it again. Try this: I like your strength, but you don't have to be strong all the time. I appreciate it when you share your weakness, too. I can handle that.
>
> *Ideal Partner:* I like your strength, but you don't have to be strong all the time. I appreciate it when you share your weakness, too. I can handle that.

---

## Assumption versus Fact

Communication is often blocked because of incorrect assumptions, and intimacy does not grow well in this environment. This exercise helps couples and family members to distinguish facts from assumptions and to label each correctly.

Direct the two partners (or the parent and child) to sit facing each other. They are to observe each other, without talking, for one minute. In each section, the first partner makes statements while the second partner listens silently. Then they switch.

1. **Fact Statements.** The partners complete the following statement ten times and then switch: "Right now it is obvious to me that. . . ."

*Example:* Right now it is obvious to me that you are wearing gold earrings. Right now it is obvious to me that you are smiling.

2. **Assumption Statements.** The partners complete the following statement ten times and then switch: "Right now, I assume that. . . ."

   *Example:* Right now I assume that you are nervous. Right now I assume that you are glad that it was my turn to go first.

3. **Fact Leading to Assumption Statements.** The partners complete the following statement ten times and then switch: "Right now, it's obvious to me that . . . and therefore I assume that. . . ."

   *Example:* Right now it is obvious to me that you are squirming in your seat, and therefore I assume that you are uncomfortable. Right now it is obvious to me that you look away when I look directly at you, and therefore I assume that you don't want to be close to me.

4. **The Unstated.** The partners complete the following statement one or more times and then switch: "The statement about me that you did not mention is. . . ."

   *Example:* The statement about me that you did not mention is that I had my hair cut. The statement about me that you did not mention is that I am really depressed.

The therapist then facilitates discussion between partners or in the group regarding the accuracy of perceptions and feelings brought up during the exercise and how the exercise might be useful in the relationship.

---

# Sex Therapy

It has been our experience that intensive sex therapy is not needed in most sexually abusive family systems. Their sexual problems are for the most part related to passive-aggressive behavior manifested during physical intimacy and to difficulties in communication. As couples gain self-esteem, learn to ask for what they want, and increase their communication skills, they report that their sexual relationship becomes more satisfying.

A technique that is nonthreatening to the couple and assists in developing communication is to have the couple give each other facial massages during a therapy session. This can also be done in a couples group.

The therapist states: "You are to give each other facial massages. Decide who is to receive a massage first. Take a full ten minutes for each massage. The partner receiving the massage is to give the other partner directions and feedback, such as 'More pressure,' 'Move in small circles,' 'That is uncomfortable.' When each person has had a facial massage, we will discuss how the experience felt for each of you."

A wealth of material can come out of the exercise: the ease or difficulty of asking for what is needed or wanted, the difficulty of trying to second-guess what a partner finds pleasurable, issues around giving and taking directions or allowing oneself to be receptive, and so on.

---

# *Note*

Balance is the key to effective couple therapy. People will often choose a partner whose style of being in the world is very different from their own. For example, one partner might be a feeler and the other a thinker.

| *Feeler* | *Thinker* |
|---|---|
| *Feels controlled by others.* | *Feels in control.* |
| Information processing is incomplete, unclear, and global. | Information processing is focused, clear, and detailed. |
| Feelings are remembered in detail, and facts are left out. | Facts are remembered in detail and feelings are left out. |
| Seeks and demands attention. | Becomes remote and rigid. |
| Interpersonal relationships are chaotic and dramatic. | Interpersonal relationships are regimented and boring. |

| *Feeler* | *Thinker* |
|----------|-----------|
| *Feels controlled by others.* | *Feels in control.* |
| Sees self as victim. | Sees self as dominant. |
| Concerned with what feels good. | Concerned with what should be done. |
| Handles anxiety with denial or depression. | Handles anxiety with intellectualization. |

When working with a couple to increase effective communication and to promote intimacy in their relationship, therapists often focus on getting the thinker to express feelings but fail to work with the equally dysfunctional style of the feeler. This aligns the therapist with one partner and against the other. This alignment raises the anxiety level of the thinker and acts to escalate defenses. Also, the feeler's style becomes reinforced. Both the positive and the negative aspects of each style need to be underlined in treatment. Each partner has something valuable to teach the other to enhance the relationship. Exercises used in therapy need to include both rational problem solving and expression of feelings.

# Bibliography

Ables, B. S. *Therapy for Couples*. San Francisco: Jossey-Bass, 1977.

Ackerman, N. W. "Preventive Implications of Family Research." In *Prevention of Mental Disorders of Children*, G. Kaplan, ed. New York: Basic Books, 1961.

American Humane Association. Unpublished data, 1983.

Anderson, L. M. and G. Shafer. "The Character-Disordered Family: A Community Treatment Model for Family Sexual Abuse." *American Journal of Orthopsychiatry* 49, no. 3 (July 1979): 436–45.

Arndt, W. G. and B. Ladd. "Brother-Sister Incest: Aversion, Guilt, and Neurosis." Psychology Department, University of Missouri, 1976.

Bateson, G. and D. Jackson. "Toward a Theory of Schizophrenia." *Behavioral Science* 1 (1956):251.

Bender, L. and A. Blau. "A Reaction of Children to Sexual Relations with Adults." *American Journal of Orthopsychiatry* 7 (1937): 500–18.

Bowen, M. "Theory in the Practice of Psychotherapy." In *Family Therapy: Theory and Practice*, P. Guerin, ed. New York: Gardner Press, 1977.

Burgess, A. W. and L. L. Holmstrom. "Sexual Trauma of Children and Adolescents: Pressure, Sex and Secrecy." *Nursing Clinics of North America* 10, no. 3 (1975): 551–63.

Burgess, A. W., L. L. Holmstrom, and M. P. McCauseland. "Child Sexual Assault by a Family Member." *Victimology: An International Journal* 2 (1977): 236–50.

Burgess, A. W., A. N. Groth, L. L. Holmstrom, and S. M. Sgroi. *Sexual Assault of Children and Adolescents*. Lexington, Mass: D. C. Heath, Lexington Books, 1978.

Butler, S. *Conspiracy of Silence: The Trauma of Incest*. San Francisco: New Glide Publications, 1978.

Cavallin, H. "Incestuous Fathers: A Clinical Report." *American Journal of Psychiatry* 122, no. 10 (1966): 1132–38.

Cormier B. M., M. Kennedy, and J. Sangowicz. "Psychodynamics of

Father-Daughter Incest." *Canadian Psychiatric Association Journal* 5, no. 7 (1962): 203.

DeFrancis, V. *Protecting the Child Victim of Sex Crimes Committed by Adults.* Denver: American Humane Association, Children's Division, ERIC, ED 055 645, 1968.

————. *Sexual Abuse of Children: Child Victims of Incest.* Denver: American Humane Association Children's Division, 1968.

Eist, H. I. and A. U. Mandel. "Family Treatment of Ongoing Incest Behavior." *Family Process* 7 (1968): 216–32.

Giaretto, H. "Humanistic Treatment of Father-Daughter Incest." In *Child Abuse and Neglect: The Family and the Community,* R. E. Helfer and C. H. Kemp, eds. Cambridge, Mass.: Ballinger, 1976.

————. *Integrated Treatment of Child Sexual Abuse.* Palo Alto: Science and Behavior Books, 1982.

Groth, A. N. and H. J. Birnbaum. "Adult Sexual Orientation and the Attraction to Underage Persons." *Archives of Sexual Behavior* 7, no. 3 (1978): 175–81.

————. *Men Who Rape: The Psychology of the Offender.* New York: Plenum, 1979.

Groth, A. N. and A. W. Burgess. "Motivational Intent in the Sexual Assault of Children." *Criminal Justice and Behavior: An International Journal of Correctional Psychology* 4 (1977): 253–64.

Gutheil, T. G. and N. C. Avery. "Multiple Overt Incest as Family Defense Against Loss." *Family Process,* 1975, pp. 105–6.

Haley, J. "Strategic Therapy When a Child is Presented as the Problem." *Journal of the American Academy of Child Psychiatry* 12 (1973): 641–59.

————. *Problem-Solving Therapy: New Strategies for Effective Family Therapy.* New York: Harper & Row, Harper Colophon Books, 1978.

Herman, J. and L. Hirschman. "Father-Daughter Incest." *Signs* 2, no. 4 (1977): 735–56.

Jackson, D. "The Question of Family Homeostasis." *Psychiatric Quarterly,* supplement 31, no. 1 (1957): 79.

Justice, B. and R. Justice. *The Broken Taboo: Sex in the Family.* New York: Human Sciences Press, 1979.

Kaufman, I. and A. Peck. "The Family Constellation and Overt Incestuous Relations Between Father and Daughter." *American Journal of Orthopsychiatry* 24 (1954): 266–79.

Kinsey, A. C., W. B. Pomeroy, C. E. Martin. *Sexual Behavior in the Human Male.* Philadelphia: Saunders, 1948.

Kinsey, A. C., W. B. Pomeroy, C. E. Martin, P. Gebhard. *Sexual Behavior in the Human Female.* Philadelphia: Saunders, 1953.

Knittle, B. and S. Tuana. "Group Therapy for Victims of Intrafamilial Sexual Abuse." *Clinical Social Work Journal* 8, no. 4 (1980): 236–42.

Lidz, T., A. Fleck, and A. Cornelison. *Schizophrenia and the Family.* New York: International Universities Press, 1965.

Lukianowicz, N. "Incest-II: Other Types of Incest." *British Journal of Psychiatry* 120 (1972): 308–13b.

Lustign, N., J. W. Dresser, S. W. Spellman and T. B. Murray. "Incest: A Family Group Survival Pattern." *Archives of General Psychiatry* 14 (1966): 31–40.

Luthman, S. and M. Kirschenbaum. *The Dynamic Family.* Palo Alto: Science and Behavior Books, 1974.

Machotka, P., F. Pittman, and K. Flomenhaft. "Incest as a Family Affair." *Family Process* 6 (1967): 98–116.

Maisch, H. *Incest.* London: Andre Deutsch, 1973.

Minuchin, S. *Families and Family Therapy.* Cambridge, Mass.: Harvard University Press, 1974.

Mirandy, J. "Preschool for Abused Children." In *The Abused Child,* H. P. Martin, ed. Cambridge, Mass.: Ballinger, 1976.

J. Gary Mitchell Film Company. *Incest: The Victim Nobody Believes.* Available from MTI Teleprograms, Inc., 3710 Commercial Ave., North Brook, IL 60062, 1975.

Nasjleti, M. "Suffering in Silence: The Male Incest Victim." *Child Welfare,* LIX, no. 5 (May 1980).

Nobile, P. Review of *Sex without Shame,* by A. Yates. *San Francisco Chronicle,* 17 May 1978, p. 21.

Peris, F. S., R. F. Hefferline, and P. Goodman. *Gestalt Therapy.* New York: Julian Press, 1951.

Rosenfeld, A. and E. H. Newberger. "Compassion Versus Control: Conceptual and Practical Pitfalls in the Broadened Definition of Child Abuse." *Journal of the American Medical Association* 4 (1977): 2086–88.

Satir, V. *Conjoint Family Therapy.* Palo Alto: Science and Behavior Books, 1977.

Sgroi, S. "Sexual Molestation of Children: The Last Frontier in Child Abuse." *Children Today* 68 (May-June 1975): 18–21, 44.

_____ . *Handbook of Clinical Intervention in Child Sexual Abuse.* Lexington, Mass: Lexington Books, 1982.

Sloane, P. and E. Karpinsky. "Effects of Incest on the Participants." *American Journal of Orthopsychiatry* 12 (October 1942): 666–73.

State of California, Department of Social Services. *Child Protective Services. Statistical Report for the Year January–December 1980.* Statistical Services Bureau, Statistical Series, CPS 2 - 1981 - 1.

_____ . *Child Protective Services Statistical Report for the Year January–December 1981.* Statistical Services Bureau, Statistical Series, CPS 2 - 1982 - 1.

Tormes, Y. *Child Victims of Incest.* Denver: American Humane Association,

Children's Division, 1968.

Weeks, R. B. "The Sexually Exploited Child." *Southern Medical Journal* 69, no. 7 (1976): 848–50.

Weinberg, K. *Incest Behavior.* New York: Citadel Press, 1955.

Weiner, J. B. "Father-Daughter Incest." *Psychiatric Quarterly* 36 (1962): 1132–38.

Wynne, L. C., I. M. Ryckoff, J. Day, and S. I. Hirsch. "Pseudomutuality in the Family Relations of Schizophrenics." *Psychiatry* 21:205–20.